Out of the Limelight

Out of the Limelight

Events, Operations, Missions
and Personalities in Israeli History

Eliyahu Sacharov

JERUSALEM ◆ NEW YORK

This book was published in Hebrew,
by Ministry of Defense Publishing House, 2000.

Translated from Hebrew by Rachel Bar Yosef.

Typesetting: Raphaël Freeman, Jerusalem Typesetting
Cover Design: Ruthie Beth-Or, Studio Paz, Jerusalem

ISBN 965-229-298-2

1　3　5　7　9　8　6　4　2

Gefen Publishing House
6 Hatzvi Street, Jerusalem 91360, Israel
972-2-538-0247
orders@gefenpublishing.com

Gefen Books
12 New Street, Hewlett, NY 11557, USA
516-295-2805
orders@gefenpublishing.com

www.israelbooks.com

Printed in Israel

Send for our free catalogue

Dedicated to my beloved wife, Tania,
my partner in times of distress and happiness,
to mark seventy years of friendship and marriage;
and to my dear Daphna Alroi and Naomi Kolitz,
Gili Alroi-Ben Horin, Ronnie Alroi-Stern and
Nivi Alroi, Ariel, Yadin and Tami Kolitz,
Tal and Uri Ben Horin

Contents

———————

Foreword

On May 15, 1948, the day after the State of Israel was declared, the Arab armies of the neighboring countries—Egypt, Jordan, Iraq, Syria, and Lebanon—invaded Israeli territory. These established armies enjoyed an absolute advantage in terms of heavy weapons and equipment. The pre-state Jewish population numbered 650,000, while its Arab population was 1.25 million, and the total population of the countries at war with Israel was 30 million. Moreover, by January 1949 (the war lasted nine months) Israel had not only managed to considerably reduce the equipment and arms gap between its army and the Arab armies, but also to triple the number of Jewish recruits. From the moment this became the case, the scales tipped in Israel's favor in terms of its military might, which then exceeded that of the neighboring armies. The explanation for this extraordinary accomplishment lies in understanding the elements of the fledgling state's Jewish community, which had been steadily developing for the preceding seventy-five years, as well as the fateful conflict with the Arab states.

As early as 1937, a report drafted by a critical British investigating committee (the Peel Commission) sought to investigate the circumstances under which the Arab revolt broke out against British mandatory rule in Palestine, and to submit its recommendations. The committee insisted that the Jewish community in Palestine was developed and could stand on its own two feet and that the Arab majority could neither overcome it nor contain it in its midst. On that basis, the committee recommended the partition of Palestine into two states: Jewish and Arab.

When the Peel Commission drafted its recommendations, the Jewish community in Palestine numbered four hundred thousand and the Arab community numbered one million. Yet these numbers did not reflect the actual proportions of power between the two communities, as the level of organization and discipline in the Jewish community surpassed immeasurably that of the Arab community. The secret of the power of the Jewish community lay in the fact that it was an organized entity. This is not to say that it was a homogenous community with an agreed-upon, united leadership. However, while it suffered—as was natural—from various ideological, ethnic, and religious rifts, most factions recognized the overriding value of national unity—particularly facing the Arab threat—and accepted the authority of the national leadership as embodied in the worldwide Zionist movement institutions and the national committee that represented Palestine's Jewish community.

The pre-state Jewish community's political leadership consistently maintained a coalition structure, ensuring the support of most Zionist powers and entities in its midst. Moreover, most of the time this coalition was propped up by the reality of a central power in the form of the labor movement, in which the best and the brightest of the pioneering personalities were concentrated, and which spawned two key mass power groups in the Jewish community: the Histadrut labor federation and the Haganah fighting force.

The Histadrut labor federation was the key power organization of the pre-state Jewish community, taking responsibility for most of its social, economic, and cultural functions. It provided absorption structures for the waves of mass immigration, and it regulated and moderated wage disputes and workplace conditions. While remaining subordinate to the overriding national interest, it ensured the maintenance of the voluntary obedience so critical to the activities of the leadership and demonstrated its ability to cope with external challenges in the absence of an established governmental structure and means of enforcement.

The Haganah was the military arm of the pre-state Jewish community. It, too, was an outgrowth of the labor movement and the Histadrut labor federation. Yet from the outset, the Haganah positioned itself as the pre-state community's overall defense organization whose ranks were open to all able young men. The Haganah's command also took on a coalition-type character similar to that of the community's political leadership, stemming from an unequivocal desire to prevent its transformation into a sectoral power and to ensure its grass roots character throughout.

In this context, it is important to point out that although the Haganah recognized the supremacy of the political echelon and submitted to it, its existence was in no way dependent on decisions of the political leadership, exactly as the existence of the pre-state community was in no way dependent on any leadership whatsoever: It was a self-generating entity that grew out of the force of the Zionist idea and the local situation in which the Jewish settlers and immigrants found themselves, beginning with the First Aliyah [wave of immigration] at the end of the nineteenth century.

In 1906, a short time after the Second Aliyah, David Green [Ben-Gurion] wrote to his father expressing his wonder at the colonies established by the immigrants of the First Aliyah:

> Every Hebrew-speaking community is a "mini Jewish state." At the head of the colony is an elected committee that manages the affairs of the colony, including administrative, economic, and legal [affairs], as if it were a government.

The young Ben-Gurion was no less awestruck by the spirit of freedom pulsing through the Jewish settlers, driving all of their activity:

> This is [authentic] Land of Israel activity, a place where there are no foreign, external forces weighing down the free development that stems from the original forces of our people's spirit…in the Diaspora, we will not be able to improve our people's lot…there, our fate is in others' hands, while here, we are autonomous.

> —David Ben-Gurion, *Memoirs* vol. 1, pp. 30–31.

In his **on-target** words, Ben-Gurion described the meaning of the metamorphosis taking place vis-à-vis the Jewish people settling the Land of Israel. Without it, we cannot understand the enthusiasm and creative burst of energy that characterized the builders of the new Jewish community in the land, the organizational capability and capacity for action that they were able to self-generate. The centuries-old fetters of external and internal oppression were cut in Palestine in one fell swoop. The status of the individual Jew in the Land of Israel was that of a free agent. Total freedom was acquired by the individual Jew upon his or her immigration to the Land of Israel, a freedom that was in no way dependent upon the prevailing physical and national circumstances, but rather stemmed directly from the Zionist idea spawning the Jew's new, revolutionary relationship between the Jew and the Land: Herein lies the key to understanding the behavior of Jews in the Land of Israel.

The Land of Israel granted the new Jew a crash pad for exploring his or her freedom. Zionism—so essential to the link between the desires and actions of free beings under one common structure—was that which provided the overall meaning. Everyone saw themselves as enlisted in the "Zionist enterprise." Everyone found meaning and legitimacy for their deeds in the Zionist context, even if on an individual basis those deeds were not aimed thereto from the outset. The great "miracle" that took place in Palestine during the period in which the new Jewish community was being shaped during the seventy years preceding the establishment of Israel, was the appearance of a democratic community through which the spirit of freedom and personal initiative pulsed. At the same time, the community was united by the sense of a common goal on behalf of which the individual was willing to harness him- or herself.

All of the great deeds performed in the Land of Israel—the waves of immigration, the land acquisitions, the forms of settlement, building an economy, establishing a political system, forming a fighting force (the Haganah)—all of these were brought about not by the leadership, but by virtue of the self-motivation of hundreds of thousands of "anonymous" individuals like Eliahu Sacharov. These were pioneers in the full sense of the word. They believed ingenuously that that they were simply following "a decree of the movement," that they were answering the leadership's "call to action at the critical hour." Yet the truth is that they were the trailblazers, those who pushed the cart forward, the initiators and the doers, those to whose deeds the success of the Zionist enterprise was mainly owed.

Yosef Weitz, a UJA functionary, gave recognition to these "anonymous individuals" as those who were making Zionist history in the Land of Israel. Weitz wrote in his journal:

> This [the Zionist enterprise] was not the work of one person or a few individuals—though there are well-known leaders and businesspeople among them—but rather the work of a group of people of the type known as the "unknown soldier," whose deeds decide the fate of the battle, yet whose fruits are named after the commander...The detached reader [of this journal] will draw from it the conclusion that had it not been for the recent work of these aforementioned anonymous individuals, the goal would not have been achieved."

—Yosef Weitz in Chavlei Nachalah / Labor Pangs of Independence / A Part of the Estate, excerpts from the journal, p. 18.

The reader of Eliahu Sacharov's book will doubtless reach the same conclusion

Yigael Eilam
Lecturer in History of Zionism and the State of Israel
The Sapir Academic College

Introduction

I joined the ranks of the Haganah when I was in high school. As a student, I was assigned to command the communications unit of the Tel Aviv Branch of the Haganah then commanded by Elimelech Zelichovich (subsequently General Avner). Upon completion of my studies, I decided to dedicate my life and my future to the Haganah.

In 1932, when I was a member of the settlers' training group at Kibbutz Na'an, Avraham Ikar, the Haganah commander of the north of the country, enlisted me to organize a counseling staff and administer a communications and signaling course. I was qualified for this assignment thanks to my experience in the communications unit where we had worked flags, heliographs, Morse Code, signal lamps and the like. The students in the course came from the kibbutzim and moshavim in the Jezreel and the Jordan Valleys. Moshav Nahalal's representative, Moshe Dayan, would later write that he considered his participation in the course to be the beginning of his career in the Haganah. As I got to know Dayan during the course, I brought his exceptional abilities to the attention of Avraham Ikar.

At the end of the course, upon the recommendations of Ikar

and Avner, the national coordinator of the Haganah, Shaul Avigur, requested to have me transferred so that I work as his personal assistant. I thus gained the privilege of working closely with Eliyahu Golomb and Dov Hoz, and to be a frequent visitor in their homes. My closeness with Eliyahu Golomb (Golomb was called "Big Eliyahu" while I was "Little Eliyahu") and my collaboration with Shaul Avigur involved me in Aliya Bet. My main job was to receive arms shipments from abroad, store the arms in central underground warehouses under the control and supervision of Jacob Feinberg, and distribute them to the settlements.

I was part of a select team responsible for this work. This team included Yaakov Feinberg, who was in charge of warehousing for Haganah headquarters in the Borochov Quarter near Tel Aviv and was the commander of the Dan district, along with Alex Steinberg and Fima Vinokur, who were the drivers of the cars that clandestinely transported the arms to the settlements. In the circumstances of those years, this activity was very dangerous, and was considered by its very nature the most classified and secret of all Haganah activities.

In 1935, I took part in the second course for platoon commanders at Kibbutz Gvat, under the command of Yaakov Dori, who would eventually become Commander-in-Chief of the Israel Defense Forces during the War of Independence, but I was forced to stop in the middle because of a mishap with an arms shipment. While the shipment was being unloaded at the Jaffa port, a barrel of cement in which arms were hidden fell and its contents scattered all over the pier. Thereupon, Avigur ordered me to drop out of the course, since a tense security situation developed and it became necessary to adopt extraordinary measures to safeguard the arms warehouses against a wave of searches by the authorities.

While I was acting as Avigur's assistant, I took an active part in the establishment of the Haganah field companies, and I was assigned to supervise training for units in the southern districts, working with Yitzhak Sadeh and Eliyahu Ben-Hur.

My career as a full-fledged Haganah worker began, then, in 1933, as Shaul Avigur's assistant. The central staff of the national headquarters at the time consisted of just the two of us, and the entire command office was contained in one room (number 33) in the building of the Worker's Committee of the Histadrut at 115 Allenby Street. Golda Meir's and David Remez's offices were in the two adjoining rooms.

From 1933 on, security activity assumed hallowed proportions—in the institutions of the Jewish settlement in Palestine, then of the state-in-the-making, and finally of the newborn state. I took part in the development and production of weapons, and I was also active in their procurement. Several of the chapters of this book focus on these two areas of my security activity.

Years ago I began to document some of my efforts towards ensuring the security of the country. I showed what I had written to many leaders of the defense establishment, past and present, to historians, scholars, and public figures, and conducted extensive correspondence with them. I saw that they responded positively to these documents, and many of my correspondents testified to the historic importance they saw in them, adding that they considered the material worthy of publication. After some hesitation, I decided to act on their advice, and I added material on other aspects of my life—people who had an influence on me, the spirit that pervaded the years of struggle for independence and the early years of the state, a spirit that has been lost and is no more. Above all, I felt an obligation to record the events and operations described in this book, because I belong to the group of the few people who still survive from the generation that worked to build the Haganah and make the necessary preparations for the War of Independence and the establishment of the IDF. I am aware that I am the last of the generation that initiated and took part in the lion's share of the events described herein and am able to tell about them firsthand.

These chapters express my vision and my connection with major personalities in the country with whom I had rather close relations and my personal involvement in various operations and events. In the preparation of this book, I enjoyed the cooperation of Israel's Ministry of Defense, in particular the ministry's deputy director-general and aide to the Minister, Haim Israeli, who encouraged me to write my memoirs and publish them. I must also give special thanks to Arye (Lova) Eliav, who also urged me to publish my memoirs. I owe gratitude to Mr. Yishai Kordova, editor in chief of the Ministry of Defense Publishing, who helped me a great deal in completing the editing of this work.

In the course of writing the book, I corresponded with various people involved in the great enterprise in which we were all partners. These letters comprise fascinating and invaluable historic documents in and of themselves, and in the words of the historian Yigael Eilam, "Many of the letters shed light on their biographical and personal qualities," both as actors in the drama presented in the book and as people whose position gives them a unique viewpoint of the events described. Unfortunately, to include all of the scores of collected letters is beyond the scope of this book, although they deal with matters intimately related to its subject matter and shed light on specific events described herein. Nevertheless, I feel obliged to thank all of my correspondents, who commented on and gave me their reactions to the drafts that I sent them. I especially want to thank the former prime minister, Shimon Peres, with whom I conducted an extensive correspondence, in the course of which he showed his open-mindedness and willingness to accept criticism.

Storage Lofts for the Haganah Files
and Underground Arms Caches

In the early 1930s, Berl Katzenelson, Israel Gorfinkel, Elisheva Kaplan (one of the leaders of the Women's Labor Movement), and Levi Shkolnik (later to become Levi Eshkol), all agreed to the request of Shaul Avigur, national coordinator of the Haganah, to install storage lofts, called *slikim* in Hebrew, in their flats. Katzenelson and Gorfinkel lived in the workers' quarter on Tel Aviv's Maza Street, while Shkolnik's residence was on Frishman. The *slikim* were intended to safeguard the files of Haganah headquarters. The files were placed in suitcases hidden among other suitcases and personal items and camouflaged. Although the *slikim* were not sophisticated installations, the files were never discovered by the British. Unfortunately, all of the documents collected in these files were destroyed on the eve of "The Black Sabbath" as part of the Haganah's preparation for the confrontation with the mandatory authorities.

It was my job to manage and secure these *slikim*, to file away the Haganah's secret documents, invoices of arms sales to settlements, and correspondence with national institutions and the Haganah district commanders.

From time to time, I was called upon to retrieve from the *slikim* material necessary for the daily functioning of the office. I recall an embarrassing incident while I was removing one of the suitcases containing Haganah files in the flat of Levi Eshkol and Elisheva Kaplan. Pulling the suitcase from its hiding place, I saw a paper fall, which at first I thought had dropped from the suitcase. Upon reading it, I saw it was a very romantic letter that Eshkol had sent to Elisheva from abroad, the opening sentences of which already made me blush. Realizing my mistake, I overcame my curiosity and returned the letter carefully to its hiding place.

The files in the *slikim* included reports and intelligence appraisals by Eliyahu "Elias" Sasson, Aharon Haim Cohen, and Ezra Danin, who were some of the senior Arabists of the political department of the Jewish Agency. Ezra Danin, of Hadera, was known for his connections with the local Arabs and had extensive ties with key people in Transjordan and other Arab countries. (Disguised as an Arab sheikh, he accompanied Golda Meir to her meetings with the Emir Abdullah in Amman on the eve of the War of Independence). There were also reports by Reuven Shiloah and Shimon Agassi of the Arab department of the executive of the Histadrut, Yehoshua Palmon, and Yosef Fein of Degania (father of Motti Hod, the commander of the Israeli Air Force during the Six Day War). Fein coordinated the purchase of weapons and intelligence gathering in Transjordan. Somewhat later, reports and intelligence appraisals were also received from the heads of the Haganah's intelligence service: Zeev Sherf, Israel Amir, Yehuda Arazi, David Shaltiel, Efraim Dekel, and Isser Be'eri.

In my many visits to the flats that had *slikim*, I transmitted information and messages from Shaul Avigur and Eliyahu Golomb to the owners of the flats.

I especially remember my conversations during that period with Berl Katzenelson, who knew me from the Magshimim pioneer camp movement of "Young Students." He showed great interest in all that was going on in the area of security, and in the state of mind of the members of my settlers' training group, which was the Na'an chapter of the Magshimim pioneer camps merged with a group of "graduates" of the "Legion" youth movement in Jerusalem. I was happy to be able to help Berl and to answer his questions. Incidentally, this was the first attempt to merge training groups of the two movements. One of the members of the Jerusalem Legion was Nachum "Sergei" Sarig, a member of Kibbutz Bet Hashita and commander of the Negev Brigade of the Palmach in the War of Independence. His beautiful wife, Tikva, was another member of the group, and they were then already boyfriend and girlfriend.

Haganah headquarters functioned as the nerve center of the organization. The district and bloc commanders, members of the national command, settlement commanders, and settlement treasurers, among others, would crowd in, waiting their turn to pour out their troubles and problems to Avigur, to ask his advice and receive his guidance.

In our office was the card file that showed where all the central arms caches were. By the 1940s, a list showing the quantities of arms and equipment in the various settlements was also maintained. The card file was hidden in *slikim*, and I would update it from time to time.

Every year, we used to conduct an inventory of all the weapons in all the settlements. Whenever weapons accumulated in the central stores, the national command would discuss and set priorities, and the arms would be distributed in accordance with their decisions. The settlements' institutions would pay for the arms in cash or promissory notes. The money was deposited in a special account at Bank Hapoalim and was kept at the disposal of the national central organization as a supplement to the basic budget allotted by the national institutions to provide the funds for the organization of the Haganah and for arms purchases.

In the settlements, the arms caches were hidden in milk vats and containers buried underground, either within the villages or outside them. In the cities, in contrast, arms were stored in other ways more suitable to urban conditions: under floors, between walls, in schools, and in factories.

Thanks to the experience I gained in the storage of arms, in 1939 the national command gave me the assignment of coordinating and leading a program for the building of ten central subterranean storage facilities, both national and regional, to hold reserves of weapons. The program was financed by a special fund set up by Ben-Gurion for this purpose, and I carried it out to its completion.

For the first time in the Haganah's existence, it had hidden stores of weapons scattered all over the country at its disposal. There were *slikim* in the Borochov Quarter, Yarkona, Nahalat Dan, Yagur, Ramat David, Yavneh, Beer Tuvia, Nahalal, and Kfar Giladi. These were of solid construction, and camouflaged to the best possible extent, using stratagems, and technical sophistication. With the exception of the Kibbutz Yagur underground warehouse, which was revealed to the British by an informer, all the *slikim* stood the exacting tests inflicted on them in the years of the struggle.

In consultation with the bloc commanders, Israel Galili—an assistant to the head of the Haganah—and I maintained the list of the whereabouts of the new caches. One cache was set up in Yarkona, on the farmstead of Avraham Shemion himself, the man who supervised the construction of all the *slikim*. We established the central *slik* of the Haganah command in the Borochov Quarter, in a natural cave that suited our objective perfectly, and in which we installed a hidden ventilation system. Another central *slik* was set up in Yagur, from which arms were distributed to the settlements in the north of the country so that we didn't have to transport them all the way from the cache in the south. Thus, by separating north from south, we minimized the danger of transporting the weapons from a great distance, as well as ensured their rapid availability.

To establish each bloc cache cost about 500 mandatory pounds, a considerable sum in those days. The investment in the two central *slikim* at Borochov and Yagur was incomparably greater for several reasons: the quantities of weapons stored there was much greater, the necessity of installing complicated ventilation systems, and the need for maximum camouflage for the openings to make them un-detectable by the British forces' magnetic detection instruments.

The *slikim* were built three to four meters underground, after we made sure that at that depth detection devices would not be able to expose the arms. And just to be on the safe side, we spread metal fragments over a large radius around the cache in order to mislead the detection devices. Very few people were involved in this project or knew the whereabouts of the *slikim*.

Building the ten *slikim* took about ten months. To outsiders curious about the building activity, we explained that we were preparing shelters that would withstand direct bomb hits, which sounded plausible with world war looming on the horizon. In some cases, we were forced to deceive children, from whom it is impossible to keep anything secret, with trumped-up stories and fabrications as to the disappearance of hundreds of cubic meters of earth dug up to build the caches.

Construction of the *slikim* was carried out by settlement mem-bers under the close technical supervision of Avraham Shemion. The bloc commander was responsible for doing the job economi-cally and efficiently and for safeguarding the secrecy of the *slikim*. When a *slik* was completed, we would officially hand its adminis-tration over to the bloc commander and end our connection and involvement with the arms stored therein.

We kept invoices and receipts for the costs of building the *sli-kim* and paid with the monies from the special fund placed at our disposal by Ben-Gurion. At predetermined times, I used to present reports on the progress of the construction and on our accounts to Israel Galili for his approval. When there was nothing left in the fund, we had to raise more money from various sources to finance the completion of the entire project.

One day, a few years before the *slikim* were built, a police search uncovered a quantity of weapons at Ben Shemen, and we saw this event as a warning that the British may have had information about the location of some of the *slikim*. Our intelligence service reports provided confirmation. In view of the danger, the national command decided to conduct a rigorous check of all the caches to determine whether they were sufficiently immune to detection. The performance of this extensive task was entrusted to a team of people most experienced in this field: Yaakov Feinberg (in charge of the central *slik* of the national command), Zvi Ben-Yaakov, Yitzhak Zeligman, and myself. Zachar Urieli was appointed coordinator of the mission.

Shaul Avigur defined the mission thus: to visit all of the settlements, accompanied by the bloc commanders, and to check whether the *slikim* met our criteria and withstood the necessary tests. We were given the authority to disqualify any *slik* that could not meet the required standards.

To help us in our work, we used a detailed questionnaire, requesting information such as: location of the *slik*, the approach to it, the structure, method of camouflage, the number of people privy to its location, their names, and so on. Together with the bloc commanders, we began our tour in all the key locations, noting all the data on the forms; this resulted in a reliable picture of each *slik*'s conditions, protection, and immunity to detection. We were forced to use this system, sitting in each settlement's office with its representative, instead of actually visiting the *slik* itself, for reasons of security and because the settlements were loath to reveal the precise location and contents of their *slikim* to us.

Upon completing our inspection of every bloc, we would pass the questionnaires, together with our comments, on to Zachar Urieli for his review. The inspection lasted about six months and included all of the settlements and cities. It did not include any details about quantities of weapons, because the settlements resisted revealing any numbers at all out of fear that this might detract from their entitlement in the national distribution in practice at that time. At the end of the inspection, it was the responsibility of the bloc commanders to improve, upgrade, and make changes, and to move a cache to a new location, if necessary.

This action was the first of its kind, and it enhanced Haganah central command's ability to supervise the local arms caches. Previously, the issue of the arms *slikim* had been the exclusive province of the settlements, and any attempt by Haganah central to intervene came up against a solid wall of resistance. Not even during the annual weapon inventories was there any way of knowing how reliable the numbers supplied by the settlements were. The occasional effort to muster weapons for common purposes (such as courses, or reinforcements for new settlements) was always met with implacable resistance. The settlements considered their weapons the apple of their eye, mostly because the supply was so scarce. More than once, Avigur was forced to visit one of the settlements personally and to lock horns with the person in charge in order to get a few weapons. With the development of the central and national units (the Field Forces, the Field Companies, and the Palmach) Haganah central realized that the settlements could or should no longer be seen as an expedient for arming and equipping these units. They also concluded that it would be necessary to set aside substantial quantities of weapons in the central stores and warehouses specifically for these purposes.

Although the national arms stores were secured and camouflaged as well as possible, we had to work night and day to move the weapons elsewhere if we suspected the security of a cache was in jeopardy.

Thus, the turning point for the security of the stores and warehouses and district caches occurred, as I have said, once the project of building the secured *slikim*, paid for by Ben-Gurion's specially-designated fund, was completed. I would receive the order and the delivery papers from Shaul Avigur or from whomever was standing in for him when he was unavailable.

Upon arrival of an arms shipment from abroad, headquarters would see to distribution: Avigur would give me a list of the settlements for which the arms were intended, and I was in charge of the distribution. Based on the list, I would plan the shipments by geographic area. When the quantity did not justify a special consignment, we would consolidate a few smaller shipments. The driver was responsible for distributing the weapons according to the removal forms and had to secure the local storekeeper's signature on a copy. We kept all of the signed forms in special files, for reference in case of any challenge or misunderstanding between headquarters and the settlements. The papers were kept in archives, which we would periodically purge.

Eliyahu Golomb, founder of the "Haganah" in 1920. He headed the organization and other defense forces until his death in 1945

Developing and Modernizing the Military Industry: Development and Production of Mortars and Testing in the Jordanian Desert

The Haganah command decided in 1934 to develop locally a 52-mm (2-inch) mortar, which would be a copy of the British model. David Leibovitz (one of the founders of Ta'as, Israel's military industry and developer of the famous Davidka of the War of Independence) was given the assignment to produce the mortar. At the time, Leibovitz was a teacher at the agricultural school at Mikveh Israel and was in charge of the workshops there. The designing of the shells was assigned to Yisrael Yoshpe, who later became Ta'as's expert in metal casting. Yoshpe specialized in casting adaptations of civilian products in the course of his work at the Pa'amon casting factory. He acquired a great deal of experience casting tens of thousands of hand grenades of three types: abrasive, Polish, and British (Mills) grenades.

We would randomly test a few dozen grenades from each production run at the Solel Boneh quarry at Migdal Tzedek. (Yosef Avidar, the head of the Jerusalem branch of the Haganah, lost a hand setting off a faulty abrasive grenade.) It was my responsibility to test a sample of grenades, and later of two- and three-inch shells, from every run, and it is no exaggeration to say that over the course of time, I exploded or shot hundreds of these products.

The barrel of the mortar was produced and processed in a modest workshop equipped with *slikim* to conceal its products in case of an emergency. At that time, the sole workshop that Ta'as had at its disposal was housed in the Levkovitz leather processing plant, near the north Tel Aviv beach. It was camouflaged as part of the leather-making process and it was called "The Aleph Institute." The plant also had a small professional staff consisting of several lathe operators, metalworkers, plane operators, shaping- and milling-machine operators, and several more workers. The spot soaking in various leather-processing chemicals gave off a noxious smell, which added insurance against unwanted visitors to the Institute.

Leibovitz and Yoshpe supervised the work, taking great pains to make sure each stage of the work was carried out with precision. They had to search tirelessly for the special thick-walled, seamless metal pipes needed for the production of the mortar barrel. The team at the workshop also prepared and produced the components for the shells' detonation devices. It is worth noting that, at that time, Ta'as's activity was limited to the production and assembly of fragmentation grenades and a small quantity of launchers for rifle-grenades, and the repair of different types of weapons.

One of the people from whose assistance Ta'as benefited, was Mr. Suhatchover (father of Major General [reserves] Amos Horev), who administered the technical laboratories and workshops of the Hebrew University of Jerusalem. From time to time, I would meet with him at the university to deliver projects to him and to pick up the finished products. A few months later came the prototype testing phase.

We sought something we lacked in western Palestine: a large, safe area for the test, because of the danger of discovery by a patrol of the police or by Arab inhabitants who might happen along. In consultation with Mossia Langotsky, one of the senior employees at the Potash Works and aide to the engineer Moshe Novomeisky (who held the concession for the production of potash), it was decided to conduct the test in a desert area east of the Dead Sea, which was then absolutely empty.

On the designated day, we loaded the mortar and shells onto the Haganah's *slik* car and set off before dawn for the Dead Sea from Tel Aviv, via Jerusalem. The vehicles of our convoy left at intervals of about fifteen minutes and included Eliyahu Golomb's red Chrysler and a few other cars.

The following people participated in the testing: Eliyahu Golomb, Shaul Avigur, Dov Hoz (head of the Histadrut's political department and liaison with the British Labor Party), David Leibovitz, Yisrael Rabin, Yisrael Yoshpe, Yosef Avidar (training coordinator and Jerusalem branch commander of the Haganah), Yaakov Feinberg (chief storekeeper), Alec Steinberg and Fima Vinokur (the drivers of the *slik* car), and myself. Mossia Langotsky waited for us at the Potash Works at the Dead Sea with a security unit and plenty of food and water. As soon as we were sure that everything was going smoothly, we unloaded the mortar and shells from the *slik* and boarded a boat that took us to the eastern coast of the Dead Sea. From there, we walked for about another hour, shouldering the equipment and baggage. (The fact that I was the youngest in the group gave me the "privilege" of carrying the barrel in the blazing heat.)

At the testing ground we immediately got to work: The security unit spread out through the area, and we took measurements, made the necessary markings, and set up the mortar. At the signal, we fired the shells at varying ranges and angles, closely tracking the stages of the firing, the trajectories, landings, and explosions. We took measurements, wrote down all the data and other findings, and examined the craters created by the shells' explosions. Each stage of the test was conducted in accordance with the planned parameters to the satisfaction of the planners and other observers.

At the conclusion of the test, we collected and cleared the area of all of the pieces and fragments of shells left after the explosions, and, following a wrap-up discussion, we prepared to head back to the boat.

All of a sudden, Golomb threw out the idea of taking advantage of our time in the Kingdom of Jordan and suggested that we visit the ancient city of Petra, which none of us had ever seen. Perhaps we ought to have been dumbstruck at such an unexpected and amazing idea, but truthfully, the surprise was not so great considering the courage, daring, and willingness to take risks so characteristic of this fascinating personality. These traits, combined with personal charm, wisdom, openness, and natural leadership ability, constituted the key to Golomb's authority and his being the greatly admired leader of the security forces before the establishment of the state.

The defense branches at that time included the Haganah; the Palmach; the Palyam; the Jewish volunteers to the British army; the units involved in the clandestine immigration effort; the Night Squadrons under the command of Captain Orde Wingate; the Jewish Paratroop Unit serving in Europe during the war years as part of the British army; the "German Unit" commanded by Shimon Avidan as part of the Palmach; the "German Unit" that operated as part of the Jewish Brigade under Yehuda Ben-Horin (Brigger); the special Haganah unit that cooperated with the British Intelligence Service in carrying out attacks and sabotage behind enemy lines in the early years of the Second World War; the unit of railroad guards commanded by Yehezkiel Sahar and Yosef Avidar; the Jewish police in the mandatory police force; the police of the Hebrew settlements, for whom Yehoshua (Josh) Gordon had responsibility on behalf of the political department of the Jewish Agency; and the group of operatives who dealt with the procurement of arms and other war material throughout the world. All of the Jewish defense branches in Palestine at the time saw in Eliyahu Golomb their natural leader and commander.

We enthusiastically agreed to the idea. We walked in the blazing desert heat, led by Mossia Langotsky relying on a map of the area and acting as guide and navigator. We arrived at Petra exhausted, but facing the magical archaeological wonder, we were awestricken and our tiredness completely disappeared. We explored the site's wadis and some of us even managed to take pictures, especially of the majestic front of the Palace of the Treasury (the Vazana). After a short rest, we set out again. We got back to the boat after many exhausting hours of walking, but elated by the complete success of the test and all the other experiences we had just shared.

After we returned, we began the purchase of raw materials and equipment necessary to set up a special production line for mortars and the production of the first series of 52-mm mortars and shells.

Production of the mortar was a milestone in the history of Ta'as. The mortar gave to the Haganah's meager arsenal a real weapons system, the first of its kind that was effective and had what was then considered a long range. It represented an invaluable reinforcement for the defense alignment of the settlements all over the country and served as the backbone of the central operational units, such as the district mobile companies, the units of the field companies, the field force, the Palmach, and others.

The experience and know-how gained by Ta'as in the production of those first mortars opened new horizons, expanded the scope of production, and served as a foundation for the development of the 81-mm mortar (3-inch), which became the heaviest weapon of the Haganah and the Palmach from 1936 to 1939, the years of the Arab Revolt. Later, at the start of the War of Independence, the 81-mm mortar became the near-standard weapon of the IDF, used in lieu of artillery, since at that time we had no large-caliber guns at all. The visionary and pioneering roles played by the founding fathers of Ta'as in its initial format—David Leibovitz, Yisrael Yoshpe, and Yisrael Rabin—deserve recognition.

In its development of the 52-mm mortar, Ta'as unquestionably climbed to new heights and went a long way toward the upturn that began with its management by Haim Slavin, an engineer, from 1937 through 1952. Slavin had emigrated from Russia and was the senior operational and engineering assistant of Rutenberg in the building of the power station at Naharayim at the Jordan River. Later he built and then managed the Reading Power Station in Tel Aviv. When he took over the management of Ta'as, his wife Mania replaced him and was appointed engineer and director of the station. Ta'as then became a cornerstone and primary source for the arming of the Haganah units.

The Haganah command gave me the assignment of working with Slavin in his reorganization and development of Ta'as. Avigur was the man responsible for Ta'as on behalf of the national command. I served as his representative. Since Slavin lacked the underground partisan experience we had gained in the Haganah, Avigur appointed me to work side-by-side with him. It was my job to represent him in his absence and to be a liaison between him and the national headquarters. I was also responsible for recruiting administrative personnel and professionals, along with performing the necessary personal and security screening. I then worked closely with, and was subordinate to, Avigur, Golomb, and later, Levi Eshkol, who replaced Avigur at national headquarters in 1940 as the person in charge of Ta'as and of arms procurement, when Avigur took over coordination of the clandestine immigration.

Slavin and myself and a small group of assistants built the first modern factories in Israel and laid the foundations for the future military industry: the MAFLAN plant for the production of submachine guns, the light Dror (a variation of the Johnson submachine gun), and mortars; the Q plant for production of light ammunition; a plant for the production of explosives and blasting materials at Sidni-Ali and Rehovot, which availed itself of the expertise of the scientists at the Weizmann Institute; the P plant for production assembly of artillery shells; and a number of plants for casting and for other products in Tel Aviv. Yosef Weitz, chairman of the Jewish National Fund, would transferred the land to us for building these plants.

The first factory of Ta'as ("Aleph")

The author

Management and workers of the Military Industries (Ta'as) in the "underground." The photograph was taken at a farewell party for the author marking his resignation [from Ta'as] in 1951

Establishing a Communications Network
and Transmitting Stations

From 1935 through 1936 Avigur, Golomb, and the Haganah's High
Command and operational echelons realized that present and future security and operational needs demanded the establishment
of a communications network and transmitting stations to connect
Haganah headquarters with the commands in the settlements and
districts and with the operatives for clandestine immigration from
Europe.

Following a careful review of possible candidates, the engineers Misha Gordin and Haim Lubin, importers and owners of a
radio shop, were invited to an interview with Golomb and Avigur,
who wanted to see if they were prepared for such an undertaking.
Golomb and Avigur explained the crucial importance of setting up
such a network and explained its role: to ensure steady communication between the settlements and the district commands, the
settlements and the district commanders connected to the Haganah
command, and the Jewish Agency in Palestine connected to the
Jewish Agency in New York and in European capitals, as well as
with the clandestine immigration operatives in Europe and on the
illegal ships on their way to Palestine. Gordin and Lubin agreed to

begin by installing a small transmitting and receiving station. In operating such a station, they sought to learn what to expect when they set up a more extensive network that would be capable of regular two-directional communication with transmitting stations in settlements, the countries in which offices for illegal immigration were based, in which emissaries were operating, and on the ships headed for Palestine and the Jewish Agency in Jerusalem with New York and European capitals.

Within a short time, Gordin and Lubin built a small, two-directional transmitting station in Lubin's house in Tel Binyamin (Ramat Gan) and a second station in Misha Gordin's flat at 50 Reiness Street in Tel Aviv. Avigur, who considered the establishment of the communications network of utmost importance, sent me to Lubin's house to observe and assist. Thus, I had the historic opportunity of participating in the operation of the Haganah's first transmitting station.

In choosing me to take part in the operation, Avigur took into account my experience in communications—my knowledge of using flags, heliographs, Morse code, signal lights, and so forth—as well as the fact that as a member of the "Pioneers' Camps" at Kibbutz Na'an, I conducted a communications and signaling course, in which representatives of the settlements in the Jezreel and Jordan Valleys participated. I remember that that first transmission was of the overture to the opera Carmen, played on a Victrola. The reception at Misha Gordin's house was clear as a bell.

On the occasion of that first transmission, the foundation was laid for a communications system that, over the years, developed into a national and intercontinental network linking the Jewish Agency offices in New York, London, and elsewhere in Europe. While I was in New York during June and July 1948, I had the opportunity of transmitting the message to Ben-Gurion and the general staff announcing the clandestine smuggling of the "Flying Fortresses" (B-17s) from the United States to Palestine. (I will discuss this historic operation later in this book.) I often think with emotion about the time I handed the message to the beautiful "Gideonite" (code name for radio broadcasters) at the transmitting station in the New York office of the Jewish Agency and of the kiss she gave me as an expression of how she felt at the success of the operation.

With the success of the experiment, a communications department was established at Haganah headquarters and was headed by Gordin, who would train and teach generations of signalers, broadcasters, and communications technicians, and established world-class transmitting stations throughout the country and abroad. In his role as director of the Haganah's communications department, Gordin was always in close touch with Golomb and Avigur. They admired him for his credibility, discretion, trustworthiness, and nobility of character, and he became one of their close confidants.

After France's surrender to Germany in the Second World War, General De Gaulle established the army of the Free French. Through Raymond Shmitlen, who had always been on very good terms with the Agency and was later to become a minister in his government, De Gaulle appealed to the Jewish Agency in London, requesting that they allow his army to establish a transmitting station in Haifa, from which various French personnel, including high-ranking army officers, could transmit messages to soldiers in the Vichy forces, which controlled Lebanon and Syria, in order to convince them to defect and join the Free French army.

With the approval of the Haganah command, the Jewish Agency, headed by David Ben-Gurion and Moshe Sharett, agreed to the French request and assigned David Hacohen to take charge of the operation. Hacohen was given the authority to represent the national institutions and to be the liaison with Free French army officers sent by De Gaulle for this purpose. Hacohen was assisted by his close aide, Meir Giron, one of the managers of the financial department of Solel Boneh, who was appointed to take charge of the station's finances and logistics, including arranging housing for the officers and maintaining daily contact with them. It was the French officers who did the broadcasting.

Gordin, assisted by George Lossin, established the station in the home of a friend of Hacohen's in Haifa. Here, too, Gordin displayed his flair for improvisation, technical know-how, and virtuosity, building the station from just the bits and pieces that he and Lossin managed to scavenge from radio shops and businesses all over the country since the war prevented importing these parts from abroad. Gordin appointed Lossin to oversee the proper operation of the station. Lossin carried out his assignment with laudable success for many months, until the station was moved to Beirut, after Lebanon and Syria were conquered by British and Australian units.

In 1946, the chief of the general staff and the Haganah command offered me Gordin's job of directing the communications department. However, for quite some time, I had already been deeply involved in bringing concealed shipments of equipment, machines, raw material, explosives, etc., from the United States to Israel, together with Slavin. This was part of the plan at Ta'as to establish modern plants for the manufacture of different types of weapons and ammunition, to prepare us, in keeping with what Ben-Gurion foresaw immediately after World War II, to cope with the challenges of building an army capable of repelling the Arab armies after the state was declared. Furthermore, my mind was occupied with ideas of renewing arms shipments from Europe. I preferred to continue with these activities and turned down the offer of the national command. Also, I was harboring the hope that I might convince the chief of the Haganah and the chief of the general staff into transferring me from organizational and administrative work into a command path in some military unit.

In 1947, Misha Gordin resigned from his job, and the management of the communications department was handed over to

Yaakov "Yan" Yanai, who continued to build the department and prepare it to become the foundation of the IDF's signal corps. After the establishment of the state, Gordin was recruited to the police by Yehezkiel Sahar, the first inspector general, where he set up the communication system for the police headquarters, the districts, subdistricts, and stations throughout the country. He directed the police communications department for many years.

The Haganah's communication system played a central role in the ability of isolated, distant, encircled settlements to stand firm and survive during the years of the Arab Revolt, World War II, and the War of Independence. Besides its operational importance, the system enabled the Haganah high command and the IDF to keep up the spirits of the settlements' defenders, and to let them know that they were not abandoned. The communications network was of vital importance for morale.

The Etzion Bloc settlements, which fought off the Egyptians for months, made a heroic stand on the eve of the establishment of the state. That serves as the perfect example of the role played by the communications network in the encouragement of the settlements' defense units, and in rushing reinforcements and airlifts to the settlements. To this day, I remember the atmosphere of gloom that prevailed in the Histadrut building, the "Red House" as we called the red-painted building (that housed the bureau of the defense minister and sections of the general staff), when the final transmission reporting the fall of the Etzion Bloc came in on the eve of the establishment of the state.

One of the Haganah's transmitting and communication stations was at Camp Yonah, north of Tel Aviv. On May 15, 1948, the day after the establishment of the state, Prime Minister David Ben-Gurion traveled to the camp in the early morning hours to deliver his historic message about the significance of the event, a message that was broadcast in the United States to the American people and the Jewish community. He was a man who did not know the meaning of fear and exposed himself to many dangers. During his journey to the airport, he was attacked by Egyptian planes, and it was only with great difficulty that Yanai, who was accompanying him, managed to get him to a safe, concealed place. I learned this during the testing of the 120-mm mortar shell in which he took part, as I will recount later in this book.

The Transfer of Haganah Headquarters to the "Kofer Hayishuv" Offices and the Start of Galili's Activity as the Chief Aide to Shaul Avigur

In 1937, the scope of the Haganah's activities widened, and the single room that we had at our disposal at the Executive Committee of the Histadrut could no longer accommodate all the workers there. Yehuda Tamir (Stopensky) and Shoshana "Shosh" Spector had joined the staff to assist me. Thus, we were forced to move to the offices of Kofer Hayishuv on Lilienblum Street, which served as a convenient and effective cover for our activities.

The burden that Shaul Avigur carried also grew tremendously until it became necessary to recruit someone to assist him who was gifted with personal and public stature sufficient for the job of chief assistant. Golomb and Avigur decided to enlist Yisrael Galili of Kibbutz Na'an for this job.

Galili was well acquainted with the Haganah's agenda and with the weighty details that preoccupied the Haganah at that time. The only concern was that people might interpret Galili's joining us as something that could upset the delicate balance that existed at

Haganah headquarters between the representatives of the Histadrut and Labor Movement and those of the civil sector.

To avoid subjecting our delicate structure to any stress, it was agreed that Galili would join the staff as an additional helper for me, with the understanding that he would work as senior assistant to Avigur. The ruse worked, and Galili quickly won the respect of the civil representatives who came to see him as Avigur's senior aide. Galili's acceptance was due in large part to his personality and his ability to gain the trust of everyone that came in contact with him.

Shortly before the Haganah headquarters' move to the Kofer Hayishuv offices, a technical department was set up, headed by Zachar Urieli, who had come to Israel from the Crimea. Zusia Shechori served as Urieli's deputy in the technical department, having served previously as a Haganah bloc commander. Tragically, the two were killed in an automobile accident when their car overturned and landed on its fabric roof. After Urieli's death, Yehoshua Globerman from Yagur was named head of the training department, and Yaakov Yanai served as secretary. Globerman was killed in October 1947 in a shooting ambush set by an Arab gang, as he was traveling from Jerusalem to Tel Aviv to receive command of the Givati Brigade. Another pillar of the department was Maccabi Mozeri, an exceptionally talented and promising operational commander, who was killed in one of the battles that broke out in 1947. The department was housed in separate offices and reported to Chief of General Staff Yaakov Dori.

A training department was also set up, which was headed by Rafael Lev, a former captain in the Austrian army who had fought in the ranks of the Schutzbund against the fascist military coup led by Austrian statesman Dollfuss. He was also one of the forty-three prisoners once held at Mizra.

There was also a department for inspection and maintenance of motor vehicles, headed by Mila Bar of Kibbutz Afikim, who was appointed traffic supervisor in the Transport Ministry after the founding of the state. Mr. Kikaion headed the accounting department until the establishment of the IDF. A medical service was founded, and was headed by two Haganah members, Dr. Shvartzman and Dr. Izmorzic. Finally, there was a special department to train guard dogs for the settlements, headed by Dr. Mentsel.

One day I had a visit from Nehemia Argov, who told me he had separated from his wife, left his kibbutz, Ein Gev, and was in need of a job. His mood was desolate, bordering on despair. I was concerned for his wellbeing and suggested that he join the staff of the National High Command. I promised I would recommend him to Golomb and Avigur. He was somewhat encouraged by this promise, but Shaul rejected my recommendation, claiming he didn't have enough work for another person. I made another attempt, this time with the Chief of the Haganah's General Staff, Yaakov Dori, and I managed to interest him in Argov as a candidate to be his secretary. Since they were not acquainted, I outlined Argov's character and qualities to Dori, and as soon as he verified my opinion with others who knew him from the kibbutz, he gave Argov the position in which he served almost until the founding of the state.

Eventually, when Ben-Gurion resigned from public duties to devote all of his time and energy to building and preparing our forces for the challenges that were to come with the UN's decision on partition and the establishment of a Jewish state, he needed a military secretary. Ben-Gurion turned to Dori, who agreed to transfer Argov to him, and until he tragically committed suicide, Argov served as Ben-Gurion's military secretary. On one of his visits with us, he met a friend of ours named Ada and they seemed to hit it off. They went out a lot together, but nothing came of their relationship. Of course, no one can know what might have been, but it is possible that if things had worked out, Nehemia Argov's life could have taken a different turn, and it is not inconceivable that his early demise could have been prevented.

Since I was a veteran worker at headquarters, some people came to see me as a shoulder to cry on, and workers would pour their hearts out to me when they experienced distress. A particularly dramatic episode concerned David Shaltiel. He had been born in Germany, was a German citizen, and carried out various arms procurement missions in Europe after the Nazis came to power. On one of his trips to Germany in 1939, he was suspected of illegal Zionist activity; he was arrested and brought to Dachau. During interrogation he was tortured, then saved from the bitter fate that awaited him when he was set free from the camp in a complicated mission.

When Shaltiel arrived in Palestine, he was a broken man. When we met, he was depressed and told me that he was out of work, and that whomever he had approached had turned him down. I felt for him and promised to bring his story to the attention of Golomb and Avigur. When they heard what a desperate frame of mind he was in, they invited him to come talk to them and then decided to assign him to the Haganah's Jordan Valley bloc command, reporting to Nahum Shadmi, the district commander. Shaltiel had served for several years in the French Foreign Legion, where he acquired basic military knowledge and experience, and would be able to perform the job well.

Shaltiel moved to Tiberias, and in one of the security incidents in which an Arab was killed, he and Avraham Daskal (Rutenberg's aide and representative at the royal court of the Emir Abdullah) were arrested and accused of the murder. Shaltiel's wife, Yehudit, who had arrived in Palestine from Europe a few days before the incident, was shaken to the core by his arrest and was mortally afraid of what was in store for him after the hell he had been through at Dachau. According to military government regulations in Palestine at the time, he and his companions would be sentenced to death. Since Yehudit didn't know any of the key figures in the Haganah or any other organization, she visited me at my home, at the end of her rope, and told me what had happened. I was recuperating from surgery then and was confined to bed, but our anxiety for David's fate was so great that I decided to go with Yehudit to Golomb, who lived on Rothschild Boulevard. In order to avoid the patrols of the British police, we went by foot. (As a result, the incision on my leg opened up, and I was taken to Beilinson Hospital to have it re-sutured.)

Key figures in the political department of the Jewish Agency and other leaders of the Yishuv joined in the effort to free Shaltiel and Daskal. After continuous efforts and the application of pressure on the authorities, they finally managed to have them set free and to save them from a military tribunal.

Shaltiel was named commander of the besieged city of Jerusalem after Yisrael Amir. Then, after the siege was broken, Moshe Dayan was appointed military commander and governor of the city and developed a close personal relationship with the legion's commander in Jerusalem, Colonel Abdallah El-Tal, who later was involved in an abortive attempt at rebellion in Jordan and managed to escape to another Arab country. Shaltiel was named IDF inspector and went on to serve as the first military attaché to the Israeli embassy in Paris.

My two-room flat on Reiness Street in Tel Aviv served as "hotel" and haven whenever our key operatives in the districts needed a place to spend the night. My wife, Tania, put up with this inconvenience. Among our guests were Moshe Dayan, Nehemia Argov, David Shaltiel, Shlomo Shamir, Emanuel Markovsky of Kfar Yehoshua, Yisrael Ben Eliyahu from Ein Harod, Uri Brenner from Maoz Haim, Isser Be'eri, and Shosh Spector, who was practically one of our family and even lived with us for a while. I remember one particular story from those days, in which Moshe Dayan and Yisrael Ben Eliyahu, both of whom were quite large, had to sleep on our couch together. My wife and I doubled up with laughter at the sight.

Another of our guests was Reuven Shiloah, who had just started working in the Histadrut Arab department. He was not married, and he spent a lot of his spare time in our company. We got him a room in a flat owned by the parents of our friend Shoshana (Rose) Litwin-Levinson, and before he met his future wife, Betty, we even introduced him to women we were friendly with, in the hope that he might "click" with one of them.

After Shiloah started to work in the political department of the Jewish Agency, we continued to meet whenever he came to Tel Aviv. In addition, as one of Ben-Gurion's and Moshe Sharett's closest aides, he initiated the establishment of the Mossad. Together with Teddy Kollek and Meir DeShalit, he developed a relationship of cooperation with the CIA in Washington.

Another of our regular houseguests was Zvi Spector, who commanded the Twenty-Three on the mission from which they never returned. Once he borrowed my motorcycle and rode it with his typical abandon. He had a bad accident and had to stay at Beilinson Hospital for a long time. He was left with a permanent limp, and my motorcycle was reduced to a pile of junk. Despite his handicap, he pleaded with Yitzhak Sadeh and David Hacohen to let him command the Twenty-Three, and after the man who had been appointed to command the mission bowed out on the eve of the sailing, Spector got the job.

Still another house guest was Yaakov "Yan" Yanai, who at the time belonged to the motorized unit of the Haganah in Jerusalem ("the roving unit"), under the command of Yitzhak Sadeh, and sustained a shoulder wound in one of the battles. Later he was appointed secretary of the Haganah's training department, headed by Yehoshua Globerman, and then secretary to Moshe Sneh, the head of the National High Command. Some of our other "customers" were Yehuda Arazi, Yitzhak Levi, Avraham Negev (commander of the southern district) of Beer Tuvia, and Shlomo Shamir. After my arrest, security considerations prevented them from coming to the flat; thus, all of a sudden, we had more room than we knew what to do with.

On the "Black Shabbat," a Saturday in June 1946 when the British set out to arrest the top leaders of the movement, several of the heads of the Haganah, including Sneh, Galili, Yitzhak Sadeh, Yosef Avidar, and others, went underground and found themselves places to hide from the searches and arrests made by the British army and police. Sneh, who was then serving as head of the Haganah National Command, was summoned by Ben-Gurion, who was then in Paris, to consult with him and to plan our response, in view of the abrupt change in the mandatory government's policy towards the leadership of the Yishuv and the commanders of the Haganah. A disguised Sneh indeed managed to slip out of the country and to join Ben-Gurion.

Sneh's place was taken by Zeev Feinstein of Ayelet Hashahar, who turned out to be a dull personality, bereft of any charisma or personal authority. The Haganah commanders quickly became aware of Feinstein's nature and personality and questioned his having been chosen, expressing their reservations about the quality and the logic of his decisions and his orders. One of his infuriating habits was to go home every day for his afternoon nap, leaving orders not to disturb him unless it was for something requiring his personal intervention. This habit made him the laughingstock of the national headquarters staff. To demonstrate our protest, Shaltiel, Yanai, Argov, and I would take turns going to Feinstein's house under the pretext of carrying a message important enough to disturb his sleep. Fortunately, the upper echelons of the Yishuv and the leaders of the Haganah soon realized that this man lacked the qualifications, experience, personal qualities, and judgment necessary for such a job, and he was replaced by Shaul Avigur, who was reappointed head of the Haganah.

Replacing Live Fragmentation Grenades with Blanks

One day in the late 1930s, I was summoned to Eliyahu Golomb's house. I found him in the company of Shaul Avigur and Israel Galili, who looked very worried. They told me that the night before, a unit of the Jewish Settlement Police had been arrested by a joint patrol of the British army and police, after a search in their patrol car revealed about twenty live fragmentation grenades, exceeding the number of weapons they were legally permitted.

The unit had been taken to police headquarters at the Russian Compound in Jerusalem to be interrogated the following morning. The grenades were deposited in the safe of the police station at Nahalal and were to be sent to Jerusalem headquarters the next day as evidence of the "crime" and as an exhibit at their trial. The regulations of the military government prevailing in Palestine at the time considered the bearing of arms without a license as the most serious of crimes. Indeed, some members of *Lehi* and *Etzel* had been given life sentences and a few were sentenced to very heavy penalties for such a crime, as was the case with a number of Arabs also found with weapons in their possession. Word of the arrests had been received from the commander of the Western

Valley District, Emanuel Markovsky of Kfar Yehoshua, by means of the regional communication station.

I had been summoned for consultation and to weigh the possible actions we might take. The objective was to neutralize the danger that the imprisoned Jewish Settlement Police unit was in, and to prevent far-reaching repercussions of British government policy as a result of this grave mishap. I suggested entering the police headquarters and replacing the live grenades with blank ones used for training, which were not included in the definition of forbidden arms and which were exact copies of the live ones. As originator of the idea, I also volunteered to carry it out. I suggested hiding the blank grenades as quickly as possible in the Haganah command's *slik* car and setting out for Nahalal without delay. The trip to Nahalal was a long one, between three and four hours, since the only existing road we could take to Haifa, and from there to Nahalal, passed through Arab towns and even cut through Nablus.

Time was of the essence, and in view of the urgent time factor and the lack of any other feasible options, my suggestion was accepted and I was given the assignment. We notified Emanuel Markovsky and Sergeant Pressman, commander of the Jewish Settlement Police in the western Jezreel Valley, who was friendly with the British sergeant in charge of the Nahalal police.

Our most complicated problem was how to reach the police station at Nahalal, which was on the Haifa-Nazareth road, and get past the roadblocks set up along the way that were manned by British and Arab police to enforce the curfew. In order to make our trip look as official as possible and to afford it some chance of success despite the nighttime curfew situation, I recruited the assistance of Sergeant Abba Fuchs, commander of the Jewish Settlement Police in the Dan region, as escort and as representative of a semi-official police body. Each time we were stopped, he explained that we had an official, urgent, and secret need to reach Haifa or Nazareth. Amazingly, we managed to make the whole trip under the cover of this magic formula, with the officially uniformed Sergeant Fuchs backing us up. Even at the checkpoint as we exited Haifa, which was staffed by the British, our explanation was accepted and we were allowed to continue on our way. But as we approached the Nahalal police station, we were stopped by a British armored car blocking the road. The officer and soldiers at that roadblock were unimpressed by our magic formula, ordered us into the courtyard of the Nahalal police, and handed us over to the station's British sergeant, who informed us that we were under arrest for violation of the curfew.

Serving at the police station were a number of Jewish policemen, who knew in advance about our expected arrival and informed Sergeant Pressman, who was the commander of the regional Jewish Settlement Police. Pressman had a close working relationship with the British sergeant; he enjoyed the Englishman's confidence and would "reward" him from time to time. He came to the station immediately, and took advantage of his ties with the British sergeant to ease the conditions of our imprisonment and to make contact with us. It was shortly before Christmas, and he managed to persuade the Englishman to drive with him to Nahalal to get the traditional turkey for the holiday. I arranged with him to delay the sergeant at Nahalal for as long as he could, to give us time to switch the grenades.

Jewish and Arab policemen were left at the station, and the deputy commander—a Jewish corporal who held the key to the safe—took charge. The Jewish police distracted the Arab police, during which interval we moved the blank grenades from the *slik* car to the safe, replacing the live grenades, which were then carefully hidden in the *slik*.

Once we had made the switch, we notified Haganah headquarters and the Jewish Agency in Jerusalem was informed immediately. The grenades were transferred to Jerusalem the following morn-

The author

ing as planned and deposited at the national police headquarters without arousing the slightest suspicion.

That same day, attorney Bernard "Dov" Joseph (governor of Jerusalem during the siege and minister of rationing and supplies after the founding of the state) presented himself to Mr. Giles, commander of the British Secret Police and protested against the arrest of the Jewish Settlement Police unit, claiming that the grenades that had been found were blanks. Joseph's claim was checked and borne out by police specialists, and the Jewish Settlement Police unit was immediately released. At the same time, Sergeant Pressman persuaded the British sergeant to release us and our car, and not to send a report about the incident to his superiors.

Returning to Golomb's house, I gave a detailed report to him and to Avigur about each phase of the operation and its results. After hearing Golomb's words of appreciation and thanks for his part in the success of the operation, Sergeant Fuchs went back to his home in the Borochov Quarter and to his job as commander of the Dan Region unit of the Jewish Settlement Police.

My First Arrest in the Struggle Against the White Paper

In May 1939, after the publication of the White Paper, the national institutions decided to express their opposition to its decrees. However, with the outbreak of World War II in September 1939, Ben-Gurion understood that the struggle against the British had to be seen within the general context of the war. He called a meeting of all newspaper editors to make clear to them the significance of this development in the Yishuv's policy and in its attitude toward the British government. If I remember correctly, this was the first time he used his historic motto: "We will fight Hitler as if there were no White Paper, and we will fight the decrees of the White Paper and the British government as if there were no war against Hitler."

At the conference it was agreed that all the Hebrew newspapers, as well as the *Palestine Post*, would publish a manifesto regarding the new policy on the first page, calling upon the entire Jewish public to join in the struggle. On the appointed day, every newspaper except for the morning paper, *Haboker*, featured the statement. As punishment for not submitting the manifesto for the approval of the military censor, the British government ordered that all the newspapers except *Haboker* be closed for ten days. The editors and the leaders of the national institutions were up in arms against the recalcitrant newspaper, and Ben-Gurion decided to warn its publisher of the likelihood of punitive measures if they did not print the manifesto the following morning. The decision was reached in the late afternoon hours, and it fell upon me to deliver the message to the newspaper's editor. Yaakov Dori sent me to Ben-Gurion's home on Keren Kayemet Boulevard in Tel Aviv to be briefed by him.

In the meantime, darkness fell and the government's curfew went into effect. The offices of the morning newspaper were on Hakishon Street, on the second floor of one of the buildings in the commercial center at the southern end of the city. To avoid the police and soldiers enforcing the curfew and manning the roadblocks, I slipped from courtyard to courtyard, through the entire length of the city until I reached the newspaper offices.

My arrival at the office at the height of the curfew took the staff completely by surprise, and they tried to keep me from meeting with the editor-in-chief, Yitzhak Ziv Av. When they saw that I was not to be put off, they let me into his office. I introduced myself, using a false name, and gave him Ben-Gurion's message, being careful not to mention his name but instead presenting the message as the decision of the national institutions. Even so, the editor understood clearly from what I said that Ben-Gurion was the authority who represented such a decision. He was furious and claimed that the paper was not obliged to obey the national institutions nor did they have moral or legal authority to take any punitive steps. While we were talking, he told me bluntly that he knew who I really was and called me by name. There was no denying it.

Having ascertained that the editor had no intention of giving to our demands, I headed back to Ben-Gurion's house the same way I had come, bypassing police and military roadblocks, and delivered a detailed report.

The following day, the manifesto did not appear in the morning paper once again. That night, a unit of the Haganah under the command of Eliyahu Cohen broke into the paper's printing house and sabotaged the presses.

As part of the struggle against the White Paper, there were huge, very well-attended demonstrations in the cities. I was collaborating very closely at that time with Yehuda Arazi, who worked on arms procurement and intelligence for the Haganah, and who was Britain's most wanted Haganah member. His picture had been distributed to all police stations and a large cash reward offered to anyone who could lead to his capture; therefore, he went underground. The two of us had a black Ford at our disposal and I would sometimes drive it with Yehuda Arazi at my side. One day, as we were driving down Ben Yehuda Street in Tel Aviv, we realized we were being followed. We tried to lose them and finally parked on Shivtei Yisrael and entered the flat of my sister-in-law, Mrs. Asherov, at 4 Hagalil (today Mapo Street), from which we could keep a watch on Shivtei Yisrael and the car.

After some time passed and we saw no sign of an ambush, we decided that one of us would go downstairs and try to get the car. I insisted on being the one to go, since, of the two of us, it was Arazi that the police wanted the most—or so I thought. I got into the car and turned on the ignition. Immediately, two British detectives who had been hiding in the yards of houses on both sides of the street jumped out and got into the car. They told me that I was under arrest and ordered me to drive to the police station on Hashachar Street. There I was questioned by Captain Wilkin and Major Morton (the British officer who had assassinated Avraham "Yair" Stern, the founder of Lehi. Wilkin and Morton headed the department of the secret police in the war against the Jewish underground.

Wilkin, whom the Jews called Wilkins, spoke fluent Hebrew and knew Yiddish as well. He used torture in his interrogations of many Jewish prisoners. The Lehi and Etzel organizations decided he had to be punished, and indeed he was eventually shot to death in Jerusalem by the *Lehi*. Morton left the country, fearing the underground would get to him as well, and continued working in another of the British colonies. In his book, *Just the Job*, he attempted to justify Yair's murder. He still lives in England today.

Wilkin interrogated me on the sabotage of *Haboker*'s printing press, on the organization of the anti-White Paper demonstrations, and on my collaboration with Yehuda Arazi. To refute my denial of involvement in the break-in at *Haboker*'s printing house, Wilkin claimed to have detailed, reliable evidence to the contrary. I understood that the source of the evidence was the editor himself, who had lodged a complaint about my "visit" and about the sabotage that followed it. Regarding my collaboration with Arazi, they used the testimony of the two British policemen who had been tailing our car, along with other intelligence they had accumulated in my police file, as evidence of our close connection. My interrogators demanded information about Arazi's whereabouts.

Although it was futile to try and deny these incontrovertible facts, I stuck to my original story, that I had nothing to do with the actions I was accused of and that I didn't know Arazi. Asked how I had obtained the car in wartime, since no cars were being imported into Palestine and private automobiles were extremely scarce, I was able to tell the truth that I had bought it from Varda Hofien, daughter of the chairman and general manager of the Anglo-Palestine Bank. The police checked and verified this fact.

After hours of questioning, my interrogators realized there was no way they were going to get any of the information they were seeking out of me. An exhaustive search of my flat also failed to produce anything incriminating. The British policemen then took me by train, in chains, to the Acre prison, and from there to the detention camp at Mizra. There I joined my fellow prisoners, Mordecai Namir, Efraim Dekel, and other Haganah members arrested following the large demonstrations against the White Paper. I was sentenced to administrative detention at Mizra under the emergency rules of protection, for an unlimited period.

In the various prisons where I was held during the periods of my internment—Acre, Jaffa, Mizra, Jerusalem, Latrun, and Bethlehem—I met Avraham "Yair" Stern and other key Lehi figures who were among the prisoners, and I became friendly with several: Eliyahu "Kshak" Amikam, Yashka Eliav (Lebstein), Matityahu Shmuelevitz, and Dr. Israel Eldad (Sheib).

Yair was an erudite man with a noble soul, somewhat withdrawn, who radiated authority and absolute dedication to his cause. Eliyahu Amikam was affable and outgoing. After his release, I set up a meeting between him and Israel Galili at my brother's home in Tel Aviv, and a lively political and ideological dialogue ensued regarding how to conduct the struggle against the British government and its objectives. I met Matityahu Shmuelevitz when he was awaiting execution in Jerusalem. I used to converse with him every morning from the prison courtyard, when I was let out for exercise. He would talk to me through the bars of his cell window facing the courtyard. As a prisoner on death row he was denied the privilege of exercising with the other prisoners. Yashka Eliav was energetic and resourceful. He even let me in on the clever plan for his dramatic escape from the prison. The governor of the prison, Captain Wilson, ordered him to install lighting around his house and little garden in preparation for Christmas, and assigned an Arab policeman to stand guard over him. While Eliav was working, he strung out an electric wire in the garden and asked the policeman to climb on a chair and hold the wire while he fastened the other end in the appropriate place. While the policeman held the wire, Eliav climbed over Captain Wilson's fence, and his Lehi cohorts, waiting there with a car, spirited him away. After a few minutes, the policeman realized that Eliav had outwitted him, and greatly alarmed, he threw down the wire and ran around, screaming in Arabic, *"Fenak ya Yashka?"* ("Yashka, where are you?"). The prison governor, hearing the shouting, immediately realized what had happened, ran to the policeman, and gave him a kick in the pants strong enough to lift him into the air. Eliav's fellow prisoners, who knew in advance about the escape plan and heard the policeman's cries, laughed hysterically.

Direct physical and interpersonal contact with each of these men impelled me to feel the profoundest respect for the idealistic fervor that coursed through their veins and for their willingness to sacrifice all. They were put to dreadful tests, far more rigorous than those any member of the Haganah was ever put to, and they often found themselves under considerable duress. I was especially impressed by Mati Shmuelevitz's stoical courage in the face of his impending execution by hanging, and his refusal to beg the High Commissioner for clemency.

These men did not reveal their hidden secrets to me nor did I disclose mine to them. The bonds between us were friendly, characteristic of members of conflicting political and ideological movements who find themselves comrades in distress. Not even the news about "The Season"* that began to filter into the prison cast the slightest shadow over our relationship.

Forty-three members of the Haganah who had been arrested during an officers' training course were imprisoned in a separate camp at Mizra. They were court-martialed, sentenced to lengthy prison terms, and, through the good offices of the national institutions, were transferred to the camp at Mizra. Some of those imprisoned were Moshe Carmel, Moshe Dayan, Rafael Lev, Yitzhak Levi, and other high-ranking Haganah members. Each morning, on their way to work at the government farm, they would pass along a path that bordered our camp. We used to wait next to the fence and chat with them as they marched. Sometimes we saw Ruth Dayan standing across the path, holding her baby, Yael, and

---

* "The Season" refers to the Haganah's activity aimed at ending the sabotage and severe attacks on British soldiers, police, and government personnel; for example, blowing up the main government offices at the King David Hotel.

if I remember correctly, she even managed to toss the baby to her husband on a few occasions.

I was released from prison after about four months—the first Haganah operative to be set free. My release accompanied the start of the cooperation between the Haganah and British military intelligence, whose purpose was to organize attacks and sabotage in enemy territory, in which I was to take part. Of those joint actions, I would mention in particular the dispatch of the Twenty-Three in 1941 to blow up the refineries in Tripoli, Lebanon, and the mined scrap ship that was sent from Turkey to a foundry near the oil wells at PloieȘti, in occupied Romania, in order to sink her in the Danube and block a traffic and transport artery vital to the German invader. Yehuda Arazi and I mined the scraps for the ship with Gelignite explosives, which we inserted into a great many of the scraps, such as radiators, transformers, and the like. We worked in a closed room, which we had rented in the Neve Sha'anan quarter, and the toxic fumes from the gelignite that were released in the room brought us nearly to the point of unconsciousness. I should also mention the delay fuses for demolition charges, which the Katzir brothers, Efraim and Aharon, developed for the British at the Weizmann Institute (the delay fuses were intended for sabotage missions against the enemy). And there were many other operations, as well.

As part of the partnership between the Haganah and British military intelligence, I participated in the establishment and the equipping of the units that were specially trained for these missions, and I was one of the small escort including David Hacohen, Yitzhak Sadeh, and Aharon Leshem, when they took their leave of the Twenty-Three as they set sail from a pier at Haifa port on the mission from which they never returned.

Major Fromer, the British leader inspector of the mission, arrived late. I can still see the image of his entry onto the boat when he left the escort. All of a sudden, he remembered the insignia on his shoulder, ripped them off dramatically, and threw them into the sea. I sometimes regret not having asked him to give them to me as a memento of that scene. I took my leave of Zvi Spector, the Haganah's mission commander; Catriel Yoffe, commander of the boat; Yitzhak Hacker, Avraham Nuriel, and the other members of the unit, with a strong embrace. In a private conversation, Spector told me of his fear that his disability would encumber him, but he was nevertheless gratified to have received this coveted assignment.

The arms with which the unit was equipped had been delivered to them by me in our *slik* car from the Haganah warehouses, because these missions had to be kept classified and secret from the British authorities and police. Their training was conducted under clandestine conditions on the premises of the "Near East Exhibition" in Tel Aviv using weapons brought from Haganah warehouses and returned there at the end of each day's exercises.

The fate of the Twenty-Three and of Major Fromer, who never returned from their mission, remains a mystery to this day, despite determined and unceasing efforts throughout the years to turn up any kind of sign or clue which might help solve the enigma.

The First Explosion
at Ta'as Takes a Heavy Toll

After Slavin was installed as general manager, Ta'as's scope was broadened and a series of new plants were added. At one of the new plants an accidental explosion occurred as a result of unskilled and careless work and killed two workers.

The manager of the plant called me in. Since the situation was extremely serious, beyond anything we had experienced up to that point, and it constituted a crisis that endangered Ta'as's very existence, I felt justified in calling in Slavin, Moshe Sneh, Yaakov Dori, Eliyahu Golomb, Shaul Avigur, and Yaakov Feinberg, commander of the Dan Region, who lived in the Borochov Quarter, not far from the stricken plant.

I approached Mr. Teiber (founder of the Zion Insurance Company), whom I knew personally and who felt close to the Haganah, and asked him to put his villa in Givat Rambam in Givatayim at our disposal for a situation monitoring room. He agreed and vacated his home. We assembled there to discuss how we could keep the news of the accident from leaking.

We met in an aura of bereavement and depression as we were overcome by sadness at the death of the two workers. Still, we knew we had to keep a cool head so as not to lose control of developments. Our primary fear was that the explosion would draw the attention of the British police and reveal the plant's existence. That is why my first emergency measure, even before the leadership convened and as soon as we finished preparing the plant for a possible visit by persons hostile to us, was to try to calm the other workers and send them home.

Golomb presided over the discussions. As we began, it was decided that I should investigate and assess the surrounding population's reaction to the explosion, whose reverberations were heard for quite a distance, to reassure the residents and prevent any unnecessary publicity. Luckily, everyone in the neighborhood was a longtime resident of the Borochov Quarter and Givatayim. Yaakov Feinberg, who lived in the area and was known as a commander in the Haganah, went with me from house to house, and once we'd explained the source of the explosion, the residents agreed to stay away from the plant and keep quiet about what had happened. We returned to the Teiber home and reported that we had managed to limit the news of the event to the residents of the immediate area alone.

Our main problem now was what to do with the bodies. We talked to some Jewish policemen and asked them to pay close attention to any incoming information. We also urged them to let us know if any news of the explosion reached the district police.

After several hours of waiting in which we assured ourselves that there were no signs of any police activity connected with the accident, we came up with the idea of burying the bodies in a settlement some distance from Tel Aviv. We decided on the Kibbutz Ramat Hakovesh, and I was assigned to go to the kibbutz to let a few of the leading members in on the secret about the accident and to ask permission to bury the bodies in their cemetery. At Ramat Hakovesh I met with veteran Haganah members Yosef Bankover and Pino Ginsburg. Upon hearing the circumstances of the tragedy and of the ramifications and dangers likely to develop from this dreadful mishap, they agreed to take it upon themselves to organize the sad mission, with all its complications. A few comrades were assigned to dig the graves in utmost secrecy, immediately after nightfall.

I went back to Teiber's house, where I reported on the preparations at Ramat Hakovesh. We still needed to figure out how to transport the bodies. Those were the days of spot checks of the few vehicles traveling at night by patrols of the British army and police. Various suggestions were made, most of which were rejected, except for one, which appeared feasible. The plan was to camouflage the bodies by putting them into fortified crates that would be able to bear the weight of oranges that would be loaded onto a truck.

The plan was accepted and I was assigned to carry it out. With Yaakov Feinberg's assistance, we located his assistant, who worked as a truck driver, and summoned him to the plant. At dusk we placed the crates with the bodies onto a truck, drove to one of the citrus groves in the area, and, with the help of two dedicated Haganah comrades, loaded as many cases of oranges as the vehicle could bear.

I decided to drive ahead in my car in order to keep an eye on the truck's progress. It was close to midnight. If I remember correctly, ours was the only truck on the road that night. It was stopped a few times by British police, but thanks to the cool demeanor of the driver, the inspections passed without incident. My car was also stopped a number of times, and the Jewish Settlement Police certificate that I carried helped get me through.

A small group of kibbutz members led by Bankover and Ginsburg was waiting for us at Ramat Hakovesh. We conducted a modest but dignified funeral, where I spoke and begged the forgiveness of the victims' families for the fact that circumstances had forced us to take the cruel step of denying them a basic human right—allowing them to take their leave of their loved ones.

At the conclusion of the ceremony, I returned to Golomb, who sent me to Golda Meir's house at the workers' residences in north Tel Aviv, to report to her in detail about the accident, its circumstances, and the steps taken by Haganah headquarters. Since these were a matter of life and death, the national command found it necessary to keep a central public figure in on the secret and to receive her backing and sharing of responsibility.

I cannot help but mention Golda's response: When she heard about the accident, an expression of profound sadness clouded her features, and I saw she was on the verge of tears. Yet her questions focused on the circumstances of the accident, on safety and protective measures, and on what the national command planned to do concerning the victims' families. I promised her that the Ta'as management and the national command would do everything possible to aid and support the families in their pain, and would offer them all the financial assistance they would need. My words reassured her, and in accordance with her wish, I informed Eliyahu Golomb of her intention to have a thorough discussion with him about the tragedy and the lessons to be learned from it.

My Car is Swept Out to Sea

During World War II, the British imposed strict surveillance on the raw materials available in Palestine to serve the military and industrial needs of the war effort. This made it difficult for Ta'as to obtain metals vital for production, and it had to get permits for the acquisition of some of the materials. It managed to get what it needed from factories that produced for the British army and for other needs recognized as vital by the authorities, except that the quantities were inadequate.

One day we learned that a British "Liberator" bomber had made a forced landing on the sands of Caesarea and the British air force had removed its weapons, bombs, and engines. As the plane was irreparable, they decided to abandon it. We in the Ta'as management decided to set up a foundry at Sdot-Yam, which was near the plane, to dismantle parts from its body and melt them down into blocks of aluminum for Ta'as' use.

We brought a coal-operated engine and an apparatus for melting to Sdot-Yam. Isser Snapiry, in charge of the foundry section of Ta'as, used to come every morning in a horse-drawn cart from Kibbutz Gan Shmuel, where there was also a foundry for hand grenades. As there was no other power source that they could connect to, Snapiry would bring coal from Gan Shmuel for the melting. Each day when he returned to the kibbutz, he would bring the day's yield with him.

Slavin, general manager of Ta'as, suggested casting the melted aluminum into molds to produce tubules for the grenade fuses, thereby eliminating the intermediate stage of recasting the blocks to form the tubules.

Kibbutz Sdot Yam supplied the labor for the dismantling of the airplane parts, including a couple who manned an observation point and provided advance warning of surprise army or police visits.

One day toward the end of 1940, Jewish sources in the British secret police informed our intelligence service, which in turn informed us, that a police and army unit was preparing for a search in Caesarea, near our foundry.

For many years, there was no pedestrian path or road access to Caesarea, the only approach being along a narrow strip of beach. It was November, the rainiest November there had been in years. The downpours were torrential, and gale-force winds were blowing in from the sea. Again and again, waves would pound onto the hardened strip of sand so that driving a car there involved taking a risk that was too great to justify under normal circumstances. But in view of the danger of a surprise visit by police and army to the Ta'as foundry, I decided to take a calculated risk and try to reach Caesarea in spite of the many warnings we got that this adventure didn't stand a chance of succeeding.

Snapiry joined me on the trip. We drove along the beach, the new Chevrolet serving as the waves' plaything. As each wave approached, we evaded it until it receded, and then we pursued it. In this way we managed to negotiate the section of beach as far as the Hadera stream. On normal days, the stream was shallow, and crossing it where it flowed into the sea and then continued along the coast to Caesarea presented no particular difficulty. The problem was that after several days of heavy rain, the "stream" had become a raging river, an Israeli Volga, and there was no way it could be crossed in a car.

As soon as we realized that attempting to cross was tantamount to suicide, we decided to turn back, but to do that we had to turn the car around, a maneuver that was practically impossible. Snapiry got out of the car to guide me and to warn me whenever a big wave was approaching, and I drove in reverse each time a wave crashed onto the shore. I tried to turn the car around before a new wave hit, but the sea wasn't cooperating. Suddenly a huge wave came in immediately after the previous one and picked the car up like a toy and carried it dozens of meters out to sea.

Frightened to death, I marshaled my remaining physical and emotional strength, and, with a last desperate effort, managed to open the car door and flee from the raging waters. The car was swallowed up by the sea, and there was no choice but to hike to Kibbutz Gan Shmuel, where, as I have said, there was another Ta'as plant and an encampment of a Palmach platoon. We were plagued now by a horrific sandstorm, and as we walked along the shore, a wind blew in from the sea with incredible force and blasted a barrage of sand against our faces that hurt as if we were being pierced by needles. We covered our faces with our coats and at last reached the road leading to Gan Shmuel.

I asked Aloni, the commander of Gan Shmuel, to accompany me to the shore, together with some of the Palmach platoon, to help me try and retrieve the car. Aloni agreed, and we drove in a kibbutz truck equipped with a number of thick ropes. Two Palmach men who were strong swimmers swam out to the car with one of the ropes and tied it to the back fender. Yet no amount of effort helped to pull the car free since it had sunk into the seabed and great quantities of sand had accumulated around the tires.

The commander and I returned to the kibbutz, loaded a tractor onto the truck, and returned to the shore. The tractor pulled the car free without any difficulty and deposited it on the shore. We loaded the car onto the truck, and brought it to Gan Shmuel.

It was close to midnight. Our families were frantic with worry, and so was Slavin. He called Galili and Golomb to ask them what steps they thought ought to be taken, and they decided that, before anything else, they needed to reassure our families. Golomb and Slavin came to my building, climbed the stairs to my fourth-story flat, and found my distraught wife. She was afraid that I had been captured again by the British police, and that due to my imprisonment of several months at Mizra in 1940, I would be held for much longer this time. While they were sitting and talking, Isser Snapiry and I walked in, barefoot, dripping water, our shoes hanging from our shoulders. We looked at each other, burst out laughing, looking like little kids returning from an adventure or a mischievous escapade.

When we told them what we'd been through, Golomb reprimanded me and told me bluntly that unjustified and unreasonable risk-taking, rather than being heroic, was irresponsible recklessness. Nevertheless, I thought I detected in his reprimand a trace of approval and understanding.

Following this incident Yaakov Dori gave me the nickname "Submarine," which I carried for a long, long time. But the nickname was nothing compared to the reaction of the commander of the Samaria district, Asher "Asherkeh" Peled, whose car it was, and who had let me use it for my "amphibian" mission. The sea water had got into the motor and caused irreversible damage. At that time, a car was a priceless possession, and Asherkeh practically tore me apart limb by limb, because the engine was totally useless and had to be replaced.

My Second Arrest

In the summer of 1943, the British arrested me for a second time on suspicion that I was taking part in organizing a network that would "remove" arms from British army warehouses in the western desert and Egypt and smuggle them in military vehicles to the Haganah warehouses. This network, organized by Yehuda Arazi, Yitzhak Levi (Arazi's deputy), and myself, acted as a kind of "arms train," and was built around five sergeants from Australia, South Africa, and New Zealand. Each sergeant had deserted his units, taking their cars with them, and remained underground in Palestine. We made contact with them through some Haganah members who had told us of the sergeants' desire to serve the Yishuv for remuneration. One of those who had made the contact and was among the network's organizers was Sheike Yarkoni, who was serving in the British fleet at the time, in a unit stationed in Haifa.

We briefed the sergeants, supplied them with bogus forms, authentic British Quartermaster Corps certificates, and references supplied by Israeli soldiers and officers stationed in the British quartermaster section in Egypt, and sent them to the central warehouses in Egypt and the western desert. They returned with truckloads of arms.

We were well aware of the risks this activity involved. Above all, we were afraid of lapses in the behavior of the sergeants when they were in Palestine. We took every possible step to prevent carelessness on their part, particularly since they had chosen to spend the large amounts of money they received for their services on luxuries, entertainment, and the Jewish women they had befriended in Palestine.

Sure enough, our fears turned out to be well founded. Two of the sergeants had been competing for the favors of a young Haifa girl. The rivalry between them reached the point that the jilted sergeant, hurt and resentful, must have felt, in the words of Samson, "Let me die with the Philistines." He went to the military police, exposed the network, and revealed to them many of the details of its activities, the types and quantities of weapons smuggled, and the identities of the ringleaders. The British secret police in Palestine passed the information on to the military intelligence headquarters in Cairo. The sergeant who had exposed the network, Stoner, was transferred to the Central British Intelligence Agency in Cairo for further interrogation.

One weapon that had been smuggled from the army warehouses in significant quantities was of a new type, which the United States had recently supplied to the Eighth Army in the western desert: 50-caliber machineguns with ammunition. For some time, a number of Jews from Palestine were serving in the British army in the Lod airport Security Guard, under the command of Lieutenant Amos Ben-Gurion. One day, long before the network was discovered, Ben-Gurion, an active Haganah member aware of our desperate shortage of arms, brought me a 50-caliber bullet to check whether we had such weapons and if we needed ammunition of this type. I checked and found that there were no weapons of that caliber in our storehouses. I informed Ben-Gurion, but the sample bullet remained in my house, for my baby daughter Dafna to play with.

I was arrested while driving my car from Jaffa to Tel Aviv after the AWOL sergeants had identified pictures of Yehuda Arazi, Yitzhak Levi, and me from a British intelligence rogues' gallery. Sergeant Day of the British secret police stopped my car, got in beside me, and directed me to drive to the offices of the secret police. I already knew Day from my first arrest. He spoke Hebrew, and I had even become "friendly" with him when he escorted me by train to the Acre prison together with another policeman.

Luckily, as we were driving to headquarters, I managed to fish my diary out of my inside pocket without Day's noticing it and throw it to the side of the road. In this little notebook were many jottings that could have verified my involvement with Ta'as and arms procurement. The diary was found by a passerby who understood its significance and brought it to the Histadrut executive offices. If the diary had been found in a body search, there is no question that the investigation would have taken on an additional, perhaps critical, direction, since what was written there included products, raw materials, names, and other details, both encrypted and unencrypted, connected with my Ta'as and arms procurement activity.

While I was being questioned, a search was conducted at my flat on Reiness Street in Tel Aviv, and the .50-caliber bullet was found in my baby daughter's toy drawer. In another drawer, the police found a 38-caliber Smith & Wesson revolver, for which I had a license, under the pretext that I belonged to the unit of bodyguards for the president of the Zionist Organization. Next to the gun was ammunition and a count of the bullets showed one in excess of what my license permitted.

While the search was going on, Yitzhak Levi, who was also wanted by the secret police, neared my house, English books tucked under his arm, since it was his custom to come to my house every day to study the language. My wife, Tanya, standing on our terrace, saw him approaching and was afraid he would fall into the hands of the police. She managed to catch his eye and signal to him to get away as quickly as possible. He understood her signals and re-treated to the underground room that my wife and I had secured for him nearby.

The first time Major Morton and Captain Wilkin, heads of the Department for War Against the Jewish Underground, had questioned me, I had denied any association with the ring that had deployed the deserting sergeants and taken the weapons from the British army warehouses in Egypt. Suddenly, Morton and Wilkin produced the bullet that had been found in my house, saying that there were no 50-caliber weapons in British army warehouses in Palestine, and that such weapons had only recently been delivered by the United States to the warehouses of the Eighth army in Egypt. They considered this bullet to be the "tip of the iceberg" of the great quantities of arms and ammunition of this caliber, and many other types of British weapons, which the sergeants had transferred to the Haganah warehouses by means of the "arms train." Once my interrogators realized that I wasn't going to cooperate with them and they would not be able to elicit from me any information that would incriminate myself or my comrades, they transferred me to solitary confinement at the Bethlehem police station. I was relieved to know that my fears that the involvement of Sheike Yarkoni, a member of the British fleet in Haifa, would be discovered, were unfounded. Apparently, there was no picture of him in the secret police files, and when he made contact with the sergeants, he made sure to be dressed as a civilian. Had he been exposed, harsh pun-ishment would have been probable in light of his British military status.

After I had been in solitary confinement for a few days without being interrogated, a colonel by the name of O'Sullivan appeared, introduced himself as a senior officer at British intelligence head-quarters in Cairo, and informed me that my case was being turned over to British intelligence. He said he had been charged with inves-tigating the smuggling of arms from the British army warehouses in Egypt by a ring organized by the Haganah. Before he started the investigation, he chatted with me in a friendly and encouraging way, telling me he was aware that my two brothers were serving as British army officers, and that my oldest brother, Yehezkiel, had been Chaim Weizmann's personal secretary before enlisting in the army. I saw in O'Sullivan's friendly approach a warning to be on my guard and not to fall into the trap he was obviously setting for me.

Seeing that I couldn't be tricked by his friendliness, he started questioning me more specifically about all of the arms procurement that had taken place in the early years of the war. At the heart of the extensive interrogation was of course the activity of the ring of AWOL sergeants (the "arms train"), which had "removed" such large amounts of weapons from army warehouses in Egypt by means of official forms and documents, both authentic and forged. O'Sullivan placed special stress on a series of rifle purchases from an Australian captain encamped with his unit in the Negev, who would use his van to transport rifles and ammunition to Hashomer Hatzair's "Kibbutz Bet" (Gvulot). The captain would get his payment either from me or from kibbutz member Yigal Margalit, the man who first made contact with him through Haganah members in Rishon Lezion.

Since our first purchase was for the purpose of getting to know him, we had been especially careful and surrounded the site of the transaction, a grove in the kibbutz, with guards. At the assigned hour on a Friday night, two Australian vans driven by the captain and his assistant arrived, and we unloaded 130 brand new rifles. We were delighted at the sight of the new weapons since we had only a few unused weapons in our warehouses at the time. Once we saw that we could trust the captain and that he really meant to do business with us, we made more deals with him. Later on, his commanders became suspicious of him, and he was sent away from Palestine, to serve in a different unit.

In the course of his interrogation, O'Sullivan accused the

Haganah of carrying out a number of raids on arms warehouses at army camps and police stations. Most of these alleged raids were fabrications designed to test my reactions. Nevertheless, one of the army base burglaries of weapons actually did take place. Yehuda Arazi had planned and led the break-in to the British army officers' school on Mount Carmel on Christmas night, 1942. The action was carried out with the cooperation of a Jewish supporter, who provided the information upon which the planning of the operation was based. The members of the unit headed by Arazi took advantage of the holiday atmosphere and drunkenness of the officers and cadets, overcame the Arab police officers, broke into the arms warehouses, and helped themselves to dozens of rifles and machine guns. A Palmach unit stood guard. The operation embarrassed army authorities and brought about a crisis in Jewish Agency-British Mandate relations.

Another of Colonel O'Sullivan's lines of investigation concerned the theft of weapons from trains going to Egypt. The investigation lasted some two weeks during which time I managed to send reports on its every detail to Haganah headquarters by means of a Jewish policeman.

My solitary confinement became a source of rumors about a cruel interrogation and torture similar to that which a few of the Etzel and Lehi detainees had undergone. My first report about O'Sullivan's investigation, which I sent from the Bethlehem police station, stated that I was being treated with as much fairness and respect as prison conditions permitted, and these fears abated.

As a result of my reports, Mordecai Macleff was instructed to cease his operations. I had close ties with Macleff in the early years of World War II. At that time, he was serving as a lieutenant in the British army in one of the units of Jewish volunteers from Palestine. This unit was charged with standing guard and securing the British army's arsenals at Tira (near Haifa), which were among the largest weapons repositories in the Middle East and a major center of installations for the maintenance of military equipment and workshops.

The unit also escorted and guarded arms being shipped by train to the British army in Egypt and to the British Eighth Army in the western desert. Most of the time, the shipments left Haifa at night. In coordination with Macleff, Arazi, his deputy Levi, and I organized a unit of Haganah members. We spread out along the railroad track near Atlit, and hid and camouflaged ourselves as well as we could. As the train approached us, the military escort under Macleff's command would throw cases of arms and ammunition from the train's windows, and our people would pick up the cases and transport them by truck to the warehouses of the National High Command.

Since the sergeants did not identify me in the police lineup and Colonel O'Sullivan could not persuade me to cooperate, I held fast to my story—a firm denial of any involvement in weapons smuggling from Egypt and in any other arms procurement operations. Although there was no substantial evidence, I was court-martialed on two charges: possession of a 50-caliber bullet and having in my home one bullet in excess of the number permitted for the 38-caliber Smith & Wesson pistol for which I had a license.

These clearly defined and trivial charges did not keep the prosecution from calling the five sergeants, who testified in great detail regarding the activity of our network. Two sergeants, Harris and Stoner, were presented as key witnesses, and identified me as one of the leaders of the network. The objections of my attorney, A.D. Goyteyn (one of the first judges of the Supreme Court after the establishment of the state) and his assertions that this testimony was irrelevant and should be disqualified from the standpoint of the rules of British justice, the law, and legal procedure, fell on the deaf ears of the panel of judges. The latter accepted the prosecution's

assertion that the 50-caliber bullet was the tip of the iceberg of
the great quantity of weapons smuggled out of the British army
warehouses in Egypt.

In his summation, the prosecution recounted in detail the
"criminal" activity of the heads of the network, of whom I was
one, the aim of which activity, according to the prosecution, was
to remove quantities of weapons from British army warehouses
fraudulently and by means of forged documents. He accused me
of making several trips to Iraq, in furtherance, he said, of illegal
Haganah aims. Israel Rokach, mayor of Tel Aviv, who testified on
my behalf as a character witness, and my two brothers, Yehezkiel
Sahar and Israel Sacharov, who were a major and a lieutenant, re-
spectively, in the British army, and who also testified, were unable
to convince the prosecution, Major Baxter, and the judges to be
lenient and to temper their strict and vindictive stance. There was
no doubt that the seven-year sentence handed down by the court
was dictated in the context of my part in the deployment of the
sergeants. Since there was no way to appeal the verdict of a court
martial, I joined other Haganah members, who had also been con-
victed of arms possession, and a few others from *Etzel* and *Lehi* who
were likewise serving jail terms in the prison in Jerusalem.

I was released in 1946, a year later than all the other Haganah
prisoners, who had been pardoned at the end of World War II.
My name was not included in the pardon, due to the objection
of the high commissioner, General Cunningham, who saw in me
an enemy of the British Mandate, with the murkiest past of all
the Haganah members he had ever managed to get his hands on.
Only when Moshe Sharett made a personal appeal to the British
colonial minister, declaring that he had known my family and me
for many years and would vouch for my allegiance to the Yishuv's
institutions, did the latter accede to Sharett's appeal and instruct
the high commissioner to release me.

One of the first people I met on the day of my unexpected release was Teddy Kollek. I remain grateful to him and his wife Tamar to this day for their extraordinarily friendly gesture: they offered their Jerusalem apartment to me and my wife for a few weeks of respite. We spent some wonderful and unforgettable days in their home after a separation that had lasted for over three years.

The author's wife in the 1930s

The Arms Ship Prepares
to Set Sail for... Beirut

In November 1947, after the UN Resolution on Partition and the establishment of a Jewish state, Arab gangs began to attack Jewish vehicles on the roads. Traffic and supplies to Jerusalem were organized in convoys with security escorts. Vehicles escorted by Haganah members with few weapons traveled almost completely exposed in the face of the armed Arabs. A few rifles plus a submachine gun were considered a treasure. The weapons shortage was getting worse and worse. The big arms shipments of rifles, machine guns, and ammunition which would arrive between April and May 1948 from Czechoslovakia in the operation called "Balak," were still a distant dream.

Things got so desperate that our arms procurement people in Palestine, at great risk, broke into a British camp to take out a few dozen rifles and several machine guns. Two boys fell in that operation. There were no other sources in Palestine for arms and ammunition acquisition.

At the time, what we then considered a huge quantity of weapons and ammunition was waiting for us in Magenta, Italy—many hundreds of rifles, machine guns, submachine guns, grenades, a few million bullets, and explosives. These arms had been gathered all over Europe by Haganah members, who were serving as soldiers and officers in the Jewish Brigade and the other Hebrew units in the British army at the end of World War ii, and had been hidden away until considerable quantities had accumulated. Then all of the arms were transferred to Magenta and assembled there. The key people in this arms procurement operation were Eliyahu Cohen, Israel Karmi, Israel Libertovsky, Maxie Cohen, Yehezkiel Sahar, Yosef Nahmias, Yosef Bankover from Ramat Hakovesh, Meir De-Shallit, Shalhevet Frayer, Moti Hod, Yosef Eitan (Eisen), Harry Jaffe, Haim Laskov, Amos Ben-Gurion, and others in the Jewish units of the British army. It was clear to us that we had to do everything possible to bring this collection of arms to Palestine. I had set up an organization that had been in operation since summer 1946, illegally shipping industrial equipment and machinery for weapons production to Palestine, which could serve as our infrastructure to bring the weapons from Italy. At the same time, Slavin and I had begun organizing illegal shipments of machinery, equipment for arms production, and strategic raw materials from the United States. Slavin and a crew of his assistants—Phil Alpert, Eli Shalit, and others—saw to purchasing the equipment in the United States and shipping it out, and my responsibility was to set up a network of "smugglers" in Palestine who would "release" these shipments from the ports and conceal them in clandestine storage rooms, mainly industrial buildings.

I set up an organization that dealt with obtaining import licenses and releasing freight at the ports. This organization included clerks in the customs administration and at Haifa port, foremen working in Haifa port on behalf of Solel Boneh, and Jewish customs agents. In view of the complexity of our undertaking, we sought the advice of Mr. Gafni, one of the governors of the Israeli State Bank, who was the highest ranking Jew in the port and custom authorities. All those I have mentioned were experts in smuggling the equipment from right under the noses of the British clerks. We learned the routines and procedures for getting import licenses from the mandatory government, we got genuine licenses issued to fictitious names, and we ordered supposedly legal and conventional equipment for them.

By means of this organization, we brought eight hundred shipments containing 2,400 tons of machinery and equipment for arms production, explosives, ammunition, and raw materials into the country for Ta'as. Import of these machines, equipment, and raw materials into Palestine was forbidden, including detonators, percussion caps, cords, fuses, shells, and explosives. We were convinced we would be able to use the same methods to bring the weapons from Italy. I explained our plans to the members of Haganah National Headquarters, trying to convince them that they could be carried out successfully. There was no doubt the "Italian" arms were crucial, but the High Command hesitated and argued as to whether bringing the arms to Palestine in the manner I suggested wasn't overly risky.

I managed to persuade Galili and Avigur first. I still had to convince Moshe Sneh, chief of the Haganah, and the other members of the High Command. They were aware of our earlier successes in smuggling large quantities of raw materials and equipment for arms production from the United States, of the methods we developed, and of the extensive network that served as the infrastructure for this activity. Nevertheless they were hesitant and claimed that if our activities were discovered, it would bring about not only the cessation of the arms shipments from Italy, but would block future arms shipments from Europe, and would even be a serious setback to shipping equipment from America. They fully recognized that it was necessary to resume the import of arms, which had ceased with the outbreak of the World War, but they thought the conditions were not yet suitable.

There was some basis for their fears, since some of the failures in past Haganah operations of this type were still fresh in our memory, in particular the weapons that were discovered in 1936 in the barrels of cement at Jaffa Port. At that time, Yehuda Arazi had sent arms that had arrived from Belgium, including rifles, machine guns, and ammunition. As the consignment was being unloaded from the ship, one of the barrels fell onto the pier, and machine guns fell out of it, instead of cement. I remember vividly the moment we received word of the mishap at the port, how Avigur dashed out and grabbed everyone in sight, and how everyone raced to the grounds of the Middle East Fair in Tel Aviv, where the barrels were being unloaded. Working feverishly, as if their lives depended on it, everyone rolled the barrels to hiding places, before the British police could arrive and seize the contraband. Following this episode, the mandatory government tightened its supervision of imported merchandise and Arab suspicions grew. As is well known, this may have contributed to the outbreak of the Arab riots of 1936.

Nevertheless, I didn't give up. I met with Sneh and with the other members of the High Command and tried to convince them that we possessed the necessary knowledge and means to smuggle the weapons into the country. I was forced to operate even using brainwashing techniques. The hardest nut to crack was the man in charge of arms procurement, Yosef Yizraeli, who was extremely conservative, hesitant, and doubt-ridden, yet was a supremely self-satisfied person, full of unjustified pride in his accomplishments. It would not be possible to start carrying our plans out without his agreement and cooperation. In the end, our relentless efforts to soften him up and the agreement that we finally obtained from the other members of the High Command forced him to withdraw his veto.

Throughout this time, more clandestine shipments flowed into the country from the United States, and every ton of equipment and raw materials unloaded at Haifa Port added weight to the case I was trying to make with the High Command. Finally my efforts bore fruit, and in 1947 Haganah headquarters decided to approve my plans and gave me the green light to carry them out.

I enlisted a few of our people who were in Italy at the time working on various missions, especially clandestine immigration. At the head of the list was Yosef Yariv (who would later become a colonel and a senior officer in the Mossad), and these people were joined by Zvi Silver and Yitzhak Shifris, whom I had dispatched from Palestine. Silver, a native Englishman with a British passport, was able to conceal the fact that he was from Palestine and could work openly, while Shifris from Kibbutz Na'an found a broad niche for his expertise: the installation of *slikim*, our ingenious hiding places in camouflaged machines. He managed the sprinkler factory at Kibbutz Na'an and fulfilled a key function in planning and installing secret openings in the ten national and regional arms warehouses for whose establishment I had been responsible at the behest of Haganah headquarters in the late 1930s. These three—Yosef Yariv, Zvi Silver, and Yitzhak Shifris—resided in Italy and acted as our operatives there.

Our representatives in Italy purchased machinery, generators, transformers, industrial containers, and other items of equipment with empty space hidden from the eye, fitted them for our purposes, filled the vacuum with weapons, and packed them for shipping. We were assisted in the purchase and adaptive redesign of the machinery by the owner of a mechanical workshop, who was one of the commanders of the Italian partisans in World War II and whose cooperation we were lucky to secure. We established a sophisticated workshop capable of carrying out varied technical tasks from converting the spaces inside the machinery into hiding places for arms and ammunition to installing hidden openings, packing cases, and so on.

The venue chosen for our activity was the Villa Fajena, a quiet Italian farm near the town of Magenta, an hour's drive from Milan. At the same time there was an agricultural training group of immigrants staying at the farm, which was also the collection site of most of the weapons gathered in Italy and other European countries by soldiers and officers in the Jewish units of the British army. For reasons of caution and secrecy, the farm was called "Aleph," the term that our people adopted for the entire operation.

Ben-Gurion decides to use Solel Boneh's import license

We had ties in Italy that helped us overcome the many obstacles that blocked our progress. One of those with whom we had dealings was a respected businessman named Senor Domino, whom we nicknamed "Yankelevich." He offered to help us through the maze of Italian laws of commerce and export, which were mired in bureaucracy and paperwork and overflowed with formal procedures.

We sent the first shipments as an experiment, but after these reached Palestine without a hitch, we decided that we were ready to significantly broaden the scope of the shipments.

It was late November 1947, the eve of the UN resolution on the partition of Palestine and the establishment of a Jewish state. We were determined to equip ourselves with arms and ammunition as quickly as possible and at any cost. In a consultation attended by Israel Galili, Yaakov Dori, Yigal Yadin (then the operations officer at the Haganah High Command), in which I also took part, it was decided to send the arms to Palestine as quickly as possible.

At about the same time as the UN resolution, the Zionist Congress in Basel reaffirmed the Biltmore Plan, which had first been accepted in May 1942 at a Zionist conference at the Biltmore Hotel in New York. At that juncture, the proportions of the Holocaust and its horrors had started becoming clear. This had been the first time the Zionist movement had issued a statement concerning the establishment of a Jewish state in the Land of Israel, and there was a widely held assumption that the plan would lead to the partition of western Palestine.

David Ben-Gurion was deeply concerned as to the response of the Arabs of Palestine, the Arab countries and their armies, who were threatening the invasion and annihilation of the Jewish community in Palestine. He was aware of the tremendous gap between the quantities of arms the Haganah had at its disposal and the quantities needed to repel the expected attacks, particularly once confrontation with the regular Arab armies would start. He telephoned us from Basel to Italy, and urged us to increase our efforts and rush the shipments of arms, explosives, and raw materials as well as any other military equipment we could get our hands on to Ta'as.

We started working on our plans, and soon the first mishap occurred. During inspections at Haifa Port, the British discovered counterfeit import licenses, which a group of smugglers were using to bring goods into the country. Though there was no connection at all between these smugglers and our activities, their methods for obtaining import licenses and ours were similar. We realized that we had to stop using fictitious names and from now on to come up with permits for actual industrial plants. Unfortunately, this was no simple matter. For one thing, imports from Italy to Palestine were very few and the Jewish industrialists had hardly any permits for the import of machinery from that country. We intended, to the extent this was possible, to avoid endangering the factory owners, in case their part in the smuggling operation should be discovered. But when we considered the matter from all aspects, we concluded that we had to get genuine import licenses, no matter how great the danger to the license-holders. We felt that any delay was likely to result in much loss of life, far too dear a price.

I found out that Solel Boneh held a license for the import of a large quantity of technical equipment from American army surplus that was sitting in Italy, including tractors, bulldozers, steamrollers, and other heavy equipment. I felt that this was the chance we had to take advantage of, and I seized it like a man who had found a treasure.

In view of the tremendous responsibility involved in using Solel Boneh's license for our purposes, I consulted Israel Galili regarding my dilemma. Galili didn't want to take upon himself the risk to Solel Boneh without authorization either, so he brought the matter to Ben-Gurion. As Galili told me afterwards, Ben-Gurion didn't hesitate for a moment and said, "No risk is so great that it can justify canceling or delaying the arms shipment."

Ben-Gurion authorized me to apply, in his name, to David Hacohen and Hillel Dan, heads of Solel Boneh, and explain what was on the balance and what the reasons were for taking such a risk. Of course they agreed immediately to our request, entrusted their import license to me, and thus the path to go ahead with our activities opened before us.

Naturally we knew it was necessary to take maximum precautions in bringing the arms to Palestine. We were well aware that if our activity in Italy was discovered, it would very likely lead to a serious political crisis and obstruct our ability to bring more weapons from Europe and other sources. Therefore it was decided that I should go to Italy to organize the operation, to personally supervise the arrangements for insuring the cargo, and to see to the final stages of the consignment.

The consignment sets out from Genoa Port

I flew to Italy on November 24, 1947. Before I left, Moshe Sneh gave me the sum of forty thousand lirot (lirot were then equivalent to pounds sterling) for a few days, for the purpose of opening a letter of credit at the Anglo-Palestine Bank, as stipulated in the import license, and I was to return this sum after the documentary credit had been opened. This was an enormous sum, a large portion of the Haganah's annual budget. Since I was late in returning the money, Sneh telephoned me and asked that I expedite the repayment. When I tried to explain the reason for the delay, he answered, "I don't care how; I want it now!" And indeed, the money was returned a week after I had obtained it.

As soon as I arrived, we received the machinery and began to fill it with rifles, machine guns, submachine guns, grenades, and ammunition. Our people knew their work, and in no time the shipment was packed and ready. At the same time, "Yankelevich" took care of all the formal steps required for getting the authorizations and the permits. Within a few days, the entire consignment was brought to the Genoa Port, from where it was to leave on its way to Palestine.

When I saw the long row of crates assembled on the wharf, I was overcome with doubt. I was afraid such a large shipment would arouse suspicion when it reached Palestine. For a moment I considered dividing it up into several smaller shipments, but ultimately the High Command's orders to bring the largest possible quantity with the greatest possible speed carried the day, and we decided to rely on our experience—if not on a miracle—hoping that everything would work out all right.

After the cargo left Genoa Port in good order I flew home with the documents necessary to receive it there. I decided to do everything possible so that it wouldn't be held up even one unnecessary day in port.

I arrived in Palestine a few days after the Arab attacks on the Jews had started. The first incident was a shooting attack on an Egged bus near Wilhelma on the way from Netanya to Jerusalem. Six people were killed and eight injured. The next day, there were seven more murder victims—three members of Kibbutz Negba and four Jews from the Tel Aviv area. The atmosphere was extremely tense, and anxiety about the future was palpable.

I returned on the day of the funeral of Yehoshua Globerman, head of the training department of the Haganah, who was killed on his way from Jerusalem to Tel Aviv to take command of the Givati Brigade. Israel Galili was participating in the funeral, and I felt it incumbent upon me to approach him. As soon as he saw me he came over to me. Galili's face, which was clouded with sorrow at the death of Globerman, lit up momentarily when he heard that the shipment was on its way. It was clear that this news brought him a little encouragement in those terrible days.

We made preparations in anticipation of the boat's arrival. We set up several contingency locations to store the machinery and unloaded the "treasures" hidden inside, but we knew the toughest obstacles were still ahead of us. This was a fast vessel, whose voyage from Genoa to Haifa port usually took between five and six days. We expected the cargo to be in our hands within three to four days. But another setback awaited us. An event taking place in a distant corner of the world while our ship was en route endangered the fate of the shipment and turned our waiting into a nightmare.

Preparations to unload the "merchandise" in Haifa under cover of fire

It was Saturday, the Sabbath. On the docks at a New Jersey port, longshoremen were loading crates of "used industrial machinery," whose destination was Palestine, onto the freighter *Executor* of the American Export Line. This was one of the equipment consignments destined for our organization, and the crates contained equipment intended for Ta'as. American Export Line's representative in Palestine was the Dizengoff-Arison and Graetz Company. Heinz Graetz, who managed the company, was married to my cousin, and he helped me more than a little with our activities.

Suddenly, one of the crates broke loose, fell onto the dock, and the wood shattered. The carpenter, Raymond Green, who was sent to repair the crate, saw inside tin boxes labeled "TNT, Engineering Corps, United States army, Trevier Gunpowder Company, Allentown, Pennsylvania." Green jumped back and shouted, "TNT! Get back!"

Thus began a very complicated affair that ultimately ended quietly, but not without causing us racing pulses and sleepless nights, because our people, attempting to smuggle a large quantity of high explosives from the New York area port to Palestine were thus violating the embargo that the United States government had placed on the export of arms and high explosives to the Middle East. The United States strictly enforced the embargo and did not take kindly to its violation. One of our fears was that this mishap would strengthen the opponents of the Partition Plan within the government who were waiting in ambush for the Zionists, and were likely to use this affair to their advantage. In addition, the shipment was not packed in accordance with American safety regulations or with suitable protective means. The commander of the New Jersey police said to reporters called to the port that a quantity of TNT sufficient to blow Jersey City to smithereens had been discovered, and immediately embellished his words: "To blow up five cities the size of Jersey City."

The news from the United States trickled in to us. The picture became clearer when Chai Issaschar returned to Palestine. Issaschar had replaced Slavin as delegation head and was responsible for purchasing and dispatching the equipment and materials on behalf of Ta'as. He reported that the explosives were being sent to Palestine under an import license of the Phoenicia plant and had been packed in a way that bore all the earmarks of our methods. It was no accident that the crates bore addresses typical of our shipments since this consignment was shipped as part of the activity of my organization. Therefore, it would be easy to trace the connection between the shipments discovered in New Jersey and those that traversed the Mediterranean.

His words fell like thunder on our ears. We knew that the British would tighten their inspections at the ports, and would not overlook our consignment either, which was due to arrive shortly after the discovery of the cargo of explosives in the United

States. But there was nothing we could do about it. The vessel was already at sea, on its way to us, and even if we wanted to hold it up or to send it back to its port of embarkation, this would not be possible.

Israel Galili and Yigal Yadin called me for an urgent consultation. They described in gloomy colors the blow that such a discovery would deal to the Haganah's plans. I knew how vital each rifle and each bullet was, and it was clear we had to do the impossible to ensure that the shipment would arrive at its destination. We decided that if the secret of the cargo was discovered, we would try to save it under fire cover. We prepared a detailed plan to force our way into the port, we studied its entrances, checked how it was guarded, and listed its weak points. We decided definitely not to shrink from any danger. In the meantime, we received more details of the mishap that had occurred in America. It turned out that other quantities of explosives destined for Palestine were discovered. The more we heard about the discoveries, the more we feared for our consignment.

On the day the ship was due to arrive, I assembled the customs employees and other port workers that we had let in on our secret. We explained the situation to them, and they expressed their willingness to help in every way they could in spite of the dangers involved. But we waited in vain. The boat didn't arrive, not on that day, nor the following days. We had no idea of the reason for the delay, but we assumed that if a catastrophe had befallen the ship, we would have heard about it.

A Month of Tense Waiting

We felt it was necessary to let one of the employees of the shipping company in Palestine in on the secret, and I turned to the company's office manager in Haifa. He spoke with the ship's owners, and after a few days of tense waiting we received the astounding answer: Due to the worsening of the situation in Palestine, the ship's routing for casting anchor in a few of the ports in the Middle East had been changed, and the last port at which the ship would arrive would be that of Haifa. The port to precede Haifa according to the new routing would be Beirut.

It is not hard to guess what we felt when we heard this. Of course there was some advantage to the ship's late arrival, since there was a chance that with the passage of time following the discoveries in the United States, the alertness of the British might abate. But we knew that our cargo was to be the first unloaded from the ship, and was blocking the way of other cargoes. We were afraid that the cargo would be taken off the ship in Beirut or some other Arab port, and if the slightest suspicion were aroused, the shipment might never reach us and might, God forbid, fall into the hands of an Arab state.

I got phone calls daily from the High Command asking when the ship would arrive. There was no answer I could give. Those were hard days: The Arabs massacred Jewish taxi passengers in Lod and a truck with unarmed passengers from Kibbutz Revivim was attacked in the Negev. The country was ablaze. News arrived daily of battles, attacks, casualties. There were hardly any weapons for defense or for sending reinforcement to isolated and besieged settlements.

A month of suspense, raw nerves, anxious consultations, and devising of fantastic plans passed. One day, the news reached the Haifa offices of the shipping company agent: The boat was due to enter Haifa Port the next day. We breathed a sigh of relief, despite the danger that still lay ahead.

The Captain Agrees to Bring the Ship to Tel Aviv Port

The discovery of the explosives in the United States caused a commotion at Haifa port. The guard there was tightened, and the port authorities received instructions to carefully check all arriving cargo. Our only recourse was to attempt to get the ship to the Tel

Aviv Port, which was under the exclusive supervision and full control of Jewish clerks, in order to unload the cargo there. I contacted Alexander Zipstein, director of the port, and told him what was about to happen. He showed his understanding and his readiness to cooperate, but he pointed out to us the many possible difficulties.

The figure of Captain Pop, the British inspector of the Jaffa and Tel Aviv ports, embodied the first danger. Pop was a martinet from whose searching eyes it would not be easy to escape. He was especially exacting in lining up what was unloaded and in the order of releasing the cargo. Most of the time he was in Jaffa, but from time to time he would make random inspections at the Tel Aviv port, and there was no way to find out the timing of these in advance.

In addition, Zipstein spelled out the problems we could expect because of the other ships anchored in Tel Aviv harbor. We insisted on being given priority and that our cargo be unloaded first, but in those days, the backlog at the Tel Aviv port was great, and some ships had been waiting for weeks to be unloaded. We had no choice but to take these difficulties in stride and hope that we would manage to overcome them.

First the ship had to be brought to Tel Aviv. The company that owned the ship had instructed the captain and its agent in Haifa to unload the cargo in the Haifa port, and there was no one with the authority to change this directive. Luckily, the company's agent in Haifa didn't cause us many problems. The manager of the agency and I boarded the ship and met with the captain, an amiable and kindly Dane. Were it not for the stress we were under, we would no doubt have enjoyed the conversation. We hinted that we would pay him a handsome sum if he agreed to bring the ship to the Tel Aviv port. He acted as if he had no idea what we were talking about, until we named a sum that was to his liking. His eyes lit up, and after we promised him that the unloading of his ship would be given preference at Tel Aviv, he agreed to take the ship there. However, in the meantime, a significant number of our crates had already been unloaded onto the barges. We again turned to the captain and, after further "persuasion," he had the crates reloaded onto the ship and sailed to Tel Aviv.

I hurried to Tel Aviv to complete all the arrangements at the port. As we were still sitting with the port management and discussing the details of the unloading of the cargo, a port worker entered and told Alexander Zipstein, "Pop is here, and he wants to check the unloading arrangements at the port." The pallor that spread across the port manager's face told us that our plan was undergoing a decisive test. We all sat frozen as Pop entered to carry out his audit. He was a tall, heavy Englishman with pink cheeks, who commanded obedience and radiated authority. Our hearts pounded. He checked and checked again, but miraculously, he didn't notice that our ship had been moved to the head of the line. Shortly after he left the port, our ship came in.

The Weapons Reach the Convoy Escorts

Captain Binyamin Liberman, who was then serving as officer in charge of traffic and unloading at the port and whom we had let in on our secret, boarded the vessel immediately to coordinate the arrangements for unloading the cargo. Our plan was to do this at nightfall so that the commotion wouldn't be as obvious. A fleet of trucks stood at the ready, making it unnecessary to leave the crates at the port, allowing each crate to be loaded onto a truck as soon as it was removed from the ship. The trucks stood along the streets near the port, and the residents of the neighborhood were filled with wonder at all the bustle on their quiet streets on a Friday night, a kind of spectacle unlike any they had ever seen before. Only a handful of port workers were in on the secret. The rest—port workers, porters, stevedores, customs inspectors—thought this was nothing other than an ordinary shipment of equipment and machinery, and that because of the backlog at the port, it had been decided to unload the shipment on Friday night. We posted people at the entrances of the port to keep an eye on, and to accompany, each vehicle that set out. The shipment's destination was the Hamat plant of Solel Boneh in Nahalat Yitzhak, where the appropriate mechanical equipment to unload the cargo was located.

As soon as the last truck was safely on its way, I hurried with the good news to Yaakov Dori. The look on his face when he heard the news is still etched on my memory, and I will never forget how moved he was. The Chief of Staff instructed me to go immediately to David Ben-Gurion's house and tell him of the successful conclusion of the operation and of the transfer of the arms to their various destinations, in accordance with the plans and lists we had prepared together with him. Unlike Dori, Ben-Gurion gave no outward sign of excitement, but it wasn't hard to imagine what he must have been feeling at that moment.

The weapons were unloaded immediately and sent to the various units, especially to the escorts of the convoys to Jerusalem. The shipment included hundreds of submachine guns, scores of machine guns, some eight hundred rifles, and over a million bullets, as well as a quantity of TNT. Today, such a quantity seems negligible but at that time we—and the fighters who got the arms—felt that heaven had sent us salvation.

The situation regarding arms supplies was so desperate that we raced to send these supplies to their destinations, and the weapons arrived at the combat units still covered with the grease that had been smeared on them for packing.

The author (at right) and Yosef (Yoske) Yariv of the Ta'as management in 1949

Era of The Brothers-in-Law,
Full of Inspiration, Great Hope and Vision

During the 1930s and 1940s four men, all related to each other, filled key roles in the life, growth, security and representation of the Yishuv to the British authorities in Palestine and the British government. These four men were Moshe Sharett, Shaul Avigur, Dov Hoz, and Eliyahu Golomb. Sharett was married to Avigur's sister, Hoz was married to Sharett's sister, Rivka Sharett, and Golomb to another Sharett sister, Ada. All four had been members of the first graduating classes of the Herzliya Gymnasium. The four brothers-in-law were to dedicate themselves to Zionism's realization and to the development and defense of the Yishuv in the land of Israel. They all saw in the Zionist enterprise the bridgehead of the Jewish people and the engine for the building of their homeland.

The Ottoman Empire ruled in Palestine until 1917. After the occupation of the country by the British army and the granting of the Mandate to Britain, the four brothers-in-law, by then young adults, all assumed key roles in the Jewish national institutions and in the Histadrut (the General Workers' Organization). Side by side with such luminaries as David Ben-Gurion, Chaim Arlosoroff, Golda Meir, Berl Katzenelson, Yitzhak Ben Zvi, Eliezer Kaplan, David

Remez, and Joseph Sprinzak, they represented Mapai, the Workers of the Land of Israel Party, in public life and also led the Yishuv in coalition with other secular parties—the General Zionists headed by Israel Rokach, Peretz Bernstein, and Yosef Sapir, and the Progressive Party under Pinchas Rosen and Yitzhak Greenbom—and the religious parties, led by Rabbi Yitzhak Meir Levin, Rabbi Judah Leib (Fishman) Maimon, and Haim Shapira.

Moshe Sharett was the head of the Jewish Agency's political department. Eliyahu Golomb, a member of the Histadrut Defense Committee, was also the Haganah representative to the national institutions and actually functioned as a de facto defense minister. Shaul Avigur, a member of Kvutzat Kinneret, who had been one of the defenders of Tel Hai, was recruited in the early 1930s to the job of national coordinator of the Haganah, replacing Yosef Hecht. His office was in the Histadrut Executive Committee Building on Tel Aviv's Allenby Street, and I was appointed as his personal assistant. The building, which had once been the Horowitz Hotel, had been bought by the Histadrut and was adjoined to the *Davar* newspaper's building. All four brothers-in-law spoke Russian, but their roots were firmly planted in Hebrew culture (Bialik, Brenner, Berdichevsky, Ginesin, and others), as well as in Jewish, general, and most particularly Russian classics. In Haganah circles they were euphemistically and affectionately called "the Mafia of the brothers-in-law," but in fact nothing could have been less Mafia-like than these four great and enlightened men, who bore the crushing weight of the daily struggle to safeguard the Yishuv's existence and to be its representatives vis-à-vis the authorities. They worked tirelessly to build defense forces to ensure the Yishuv's physical existence, which was confronted by an ever more aggressive Arab national movement and scheming to annihilate Jewish settlement in Palestine.

The brothers-in-law were on uncommonly warm and cooperative terms. As is fitting for leaders filled with a sense of mission, they left their mark everywhere. Their personalities and idealistic fervor exerted its influence on the youth movements, Haganah members, educational institutions, and public and political life in the Yishuv. In fact it was they, led by Ben-Gurion and Berl Katzenelson, who were in the vanguard of the Yishuv's struggle, and they were among those who shaped the generation. The discerning eye will recognize in their personalities and behavior the buds of the unique Israeli ethos. The principle of "After me!", the comradeship of fighters, the refusal to abandon the wounded or to leave the bodies of brothers-in-arms who had fallen on the battlefield; and honest reporting, even in cases of failure—these are the values that embody this ethos, which became the basic code of the Haganah, the Palmach, Etzel, and Lehi, and later the Israel Defense Forces. Their names became the personification of integrity, the antithesis of egoism, ambition, domination, and lust for power, and they enjoyed the boundless trust of all their subordinates.

Ben-Gurion was the dominant personality in those decades, and was a man who stood head and shoulders above every other public figure. He and Berl Katznelson were the guiding lights, and the kibbutz movements, the Histadrut, the religious Zionist move-ment, and much of the civilian population constituted the vanguard promoting Zionism and the building of the state.

It was my great fortune and privilege to work closely with these men, and to this day I remember vividly Friday nights in the meeting rooms of the *chugim* (activity groups), pioneers camps at Tel Aviv's Herzliya Gymnasium, where they would speak. Noach Mozes, the son of the founder of the *Yediot Acharonot* newspaper, was a member of the *chugim* while studying at the Herzliya Gymna-sium, and participated in the movement's various activities. Moshe Sharett would sing to us in delightful evenings of Turkish songs and join enthusiastically in the group singing. There was nothing surprising about his lovely voice and his ear for music, since the whole Sharett family was well known for its love of music and its deeply rooted musical culture. Moshe's brother, Yehuda Sharett, a member of Kibbutz Yagur, was a gifted and popular composer and choir conductor. His sisters Rivka and Geula (the latter a member of Kibbutz Givat Brenner) were talented pianists: Rivka was also a piano teacher.

To this day I remember my visits at the home of Dov and Rivka Hoz and the sounds that emanated from their flat that would embrace me even before I entered. I especially loved Johann Sebastian Bach's "Preludes" and "Fugues" from the first book of his *Well-Tempered Clavier*, the "Impromptu" (No. 90 in the Deutsch Catalog) by Schubert, and Beethoven's "Appassionata" (Opus 57) and "Tempest" (Number 17) Sonatas. Nothing enchants like the art of music with its ideal of total, infinite beauty, from which spring the longing for the transcendent in the depths of man's soul, the sublime, and the noble, and the striving for perfection. The playing mesmerized me, and I sought excuses to extend my visits to the Hoz home as much as possible. During my imprisonment, in times of depression and sadness—and such times were many—I would find myself thinking painfully of those magical moments. At times of distress I longed to listen to the music that was not to be heard in prison, and I would have given the world for a few hours of music to satisfy my craving. There is nothing like music to bring remedy and balm to the sick and painful heart, to enable the soul to rejoice and the heart to pray.

Music was literally in the blood of Sharett's family, and part of the family's heritage. After all, in time, Harai Golomb, Eliyahu's son, became a renowned musicologist, a lecturer, commentator, and music critic.

These people were among the leaders of the Yishuv and, later, the state under Ben-Gurion. After Israel was founded, Ben-Gurion nurtured his young aides: Teddy Kollek, Shimon Peres, Moshe Dayan, Yitzhak Navon, Ehud Avriel, Aryeh Bahir of Kibbutz Afikim, and Giora Josephthal. They were part of a magnificent reserve of leadership, which also included Golda Meir, Yitzhak Ben Zvi, Levi Eshkol, Eliezer Kaplan, the lawyer Haim Zadok, Yitzhak Ben Aharon, Pinhas Sapir, Zalman (Ziama) Aranne, Yigal Allon, Israel Galili, Moshe Carmel, Yitzhak Rabin, and Israel Guri (Gorfinkel), who served as Chairman of the Finance Committee during several of the early Knesset terms and was considered the epitome of political and personal integrity (one of the *slikim* for the safekeeping of Haganah files had been installed in his home). They would have considered it a perversity to even mention hiring someone to handle public relations, or an image advisor, or even a spokesman for them. Many of them didn't even have a secretary or personal aides, not to mention a car. They performed leadership roles in the areas of diplomacy, economics, social issues, settlement, culture, and the military. They were prime ministers, ministers of defense, foreign affairs, the treasury, ministers dealing with economics, army commanders, and Knesset members. Some were elected presidents of the state. Not all of them agreed with Ben-Gurion. There were more than a few controversies, involving bitter ideological and political opponents—Yaakov Hazan, Meir Ya'ari, Yitzhak Tabenkin, Yitzhak Ben Aharon, Israel Galili, Yigal Allon, Aharon Zisling, and others. But all revered Ben-Gurion and accepted his leadership and his security decrees as a phenomenon of nature.

If the term "elite" had not been contaminated of late by boorish and ignorant politicians, we might unhesitatingly see in this group of people who were active in political life, as well as others in the fields of literature, poetry, music, art, higher education, economics, and law, a classic "elite" in the highest sense of the word, as is common practice among cultured nations and peoples.

Most of them were people of great spiritual and moral stature, and because of their modest, near-Spartan lifestyles, they served as role models. To the above list we need not hesitate to add the leaders of the opposition at that time: Menahem Begin, David Raziel, Avraham Stern, Yitzhak Shamir, Natan Friedman-Yellin, Dr.

Israel Eldad (Scheib), the leaders of the religious Zionists, and other thinkers with consistent, cogent ideologies. The great majority of these did not seek out the wealthy or the aristocratic for money for their personal needs or for their election campaigns, and they were not interested in their closeness or their patronage. Their ties with such people arose solely from their efforts to interest them in investing their money in the economy and in funding and nurturing industries in depressed areas and public projects undertaken for the wellbeing of all strata of society. They were aware of the inherent dangers of capital and politics being too closely linked, fearing that such proximity could be the seed of calamity and cast a shadow over their moves, decisions, and appointments, even if their motives were the purest and above all suspicion. Political leaders today (as in recent decades) would do themselves and the country well if they were to emulate these historic leaders. They would save themselves embarrassing and scandalous mishaps and complications that cast doubt on their integrity and the purity of their intentions, if this approach and worldview were to guide them, as it did those that came before them.

I cannot imagine the leaders of the Yishuv falling prey to the charms of the spotlight and television, dogged by a camera wherever they went. The nurturing of a personality cult is foreign to the spirit of Judaism and the Israeli ethos. I have observed government leaders in other democratic countries, and I have never found there anything resembling what we may see here. Our historic leaders showed the greatest respect and esteem for rabbis and religious leaders without effacing themselves, bowing down to and worshiping them; they did not kiss their hands or ask for their blessings. They dealt with religious fanatics, including those that negate Zionism, on an intellectual and cultural level. In a debate with Ben-Gurion, the Hazon Ish said that a loaded cart should be given right-of-way on a narrow bridge if the cart coming from the opposite direction is empty. The purpose of this allegory was to graphically represent the spiritual and ethical superiority of ultra-Orthodox Judaism over Zionism and secular Jewish society. To the best of my knowledge, this example is specious, since the Zionist movement and secular Israeli society are not comparable to an empty cart. The opposite is the case: The cart is filled to the brim with philosophers and thinkers of no less stature than that of the great rabbis, rich in spiritual and material assets—the historic enterprise of the revival of the Jewish people and their return to the stage of history, the rebirth of the Hebrew language, the establishment and building of the Jewish state, the ingathering of the exiles, the building of a culture, society, and Israeli entity.

Yet the wealth of benefits that may be inherent in religious life do not prevent vicious attacks on the institutions of democratic government—the justice system, the Supreme Court, law enforcement, and so on. And that not sufficing, there are religious sectors which bend over backwards, sometimes resorting to violence, to impose on the secular population their reactionary social worldview and their customs, dress, and way of life, brought with them from the Diaspora, which they continue to embrace as if they were dealing with sacred values. The Diaspora and the life in the ghetto that they hold so dear were what brought about the atrophy of the soul of the people, wrenched them from their roots and history, and distorted their ideals and values.

Moshe Sharett

Moshe Sharett left his deep imprint on Israeli and Jewish history by establishing the Jewish units and the Jewish Combat Brigade within the British army in World War II. This great historic enterprise would never have come to pass were it not for Sharett's determination and zeal and his indefatigable lobbying of the British government, fortified by Dr. Chaim Weizmann's exertion of his considerable influence on Churchill and the ministers of the British cabinet. There is no overstating the spirit of enthusiasm and volunteerism that he and the Yishuv leadership managed to instill in the youth of the nation, encouraging them to enlist in the various Jewish units in the British army, and especially in the Jewish Combat Brigade, in light of the struggle against the White Paper and the crisis in relations with the Mandatory authorities. Those who evaded service found themselves alienated and in disgrace. Those active in the Haganah, Palmach, and other units, whose enlistment the national institutions decided to prevent in favor of their work for the security of the Yishuv, were given special certificates to keep them from being considered dodgers.

Moshe Sharett spoke fluent Hebrew, English, Turkish, Arabic, French, German, and other languages. His eloquence was well known, and his ear was sensitive to any mispronunciation in these languages. In one typical instance, when he was prime minister, he telephoned a radio announcer to correct his pronunciation of the Turkish name Echevit, which he had not enunciated correctly in his broadcast.

His speeches were masterpieces, their wording brilliant and perfect, and his language rich and magnificent. That may be the reason that, more often than not, what he was saying was overshadowed by the phraseology. David Ben-Gurion's oratory style was different. His speeches were also works of art, but their greatness lay not in their semantic virtuosity but in their content, their authenticity, the resolve of their social and political outlook, their prophetic and biblical pathos, and the potency of the ideas and messages embodied in them.

Moshe Sneh was another gifted orator. His speeches exemplified a gift for profound analysis, an outstanding ability to persuade, and a crystal clear vision of politics and security in all things connected with the Yishuv and the Zionist movement's handling of the many challenges facing them. On any path he chose to walk, he believed in his vision and defended it vigorously. He and his wife Hanna, a tremendous personality in her own right, were very close friends of Eliyahu Golomb, a friendship that lasted until Golomb's death in 1945.

Moshe Sharett was the central figure working tirelessly at the United Nations to induce the representatives of the General Assembly countries and their governments to support the resolution for partition and for the establishment of a Jewish state in November 1947. Sharett and his partner, the determined Golda Meir, together with their team consisting of Abba Eban, Eliyahu Eilat, Walter Eytan, Gideon Rafael, Harry Beilin, Michael Comay, Morris Fisher, Reggie Kidron, and others, worked night and day to painstakingly forge ties with the heads of delegations of the United Nation member nations. They applied various kinds of pressure and persuasion, including a meeting that they set up between Chaim Weizmann and President Truman on the eve of the decisive General Assembly vote, and they galvanized all possible Jewish influence in the Diaspora in support of the resolution.

Sharett labored mightily to foil the attempts of United States Secretary of State George Marshall and the pro-Arab lobby in the State Department and the White House to reverse Truman's decision to support the Partition Plan. He stood firm when Marshall tried, in a personal conversation containing a veiled threat and intimidation, to convince him that to go through with the plan would be to bring about the destruction of the Yishuv in the Land of Israel. He even turned down an offer to fly him to Palestine for this purpose in the president's private plane. His position was influenced largely by Ben-Gurion's unwavering policy and solid faith, which stood rock-solid in the face of the tremendous threats and pressures, from home and abroad, to delay the decision to establish the state on May 15, 1948. The decision to proclaim the birth of the Jewish state on that date was a flame in his very being, and he swept along with him many who were vacillating, although in the decisive vote among the Yishuv's leadership, a number of people voted against establishing the state at that time. Ben-Gurion was driven by his deep conviction that Jewish history was presenting the people with a once-in-a-lifetime opportunity, which, if missed, would be an irreversible historic mistake and an eternal source of calamity.

I had the opportunity to observe Sharett in action and to hear about his struggles directly from his mouth when I met with him at the Essex House and other hotels where he used to stay in New York. I met with him from time to time to give him detailed reports on my activities in the United States related to the delivery of equipment and machinery for arms production purchased from American factories that had switched to civilian production at the end of the war, and on assistance we received from key people in the Jewish community and in the American economy, as well as on the operation in which the "Flying Fortresses" (B-17) were flown to Palestine.

Sharett's personal, political, and public stature did not always serve him well. He was forced to resign from the posts of Israel's foreign minister and later prime minister against the background of a serious dispute between him and Ben-Gurion, which arose from their opposing views on the shaping of Israeli policy with respect to its relations with the Arab states. I think it was a mistake on the part of his party and large segments of the population that supported Ben-Gurion's pro-active defense policy towards the enemy states, to consider Sharett and his views an obstacle to the implementation of their policy. However, I must confess that at the time I was also among those who sided with Ben-Gurion's political and security views. I completely identified with his path then, and I still feel that his policy was correct and perhaps even unavoidable for the entrenchment of the state's existence in the circumstances prevailing.

Moshe Sharett believed in seeking ways to temper the hostility of the Arab states, out of a profound belief that diplomacy was preferable to confrontation and military struggle. He never questioned the need to strengthen the IDF, but he felt that military force should be used only as a last resort. In the mood of that time, he was almost alone in this worldview among the country and party leadership. However, as years passed and we learned the lessons of war, not all of which were unavoidable, we began to see his political point of view in a new light, and many of his opponents and party leaders started to adopt his theory regarding the necessity of breaking the cycle of violence and creating a basis for compromise and co-existence with the countries of the region. Some went so far as to repent and acknowledged that Sharett's political approach had been the correct one.

The course of history reflected Sharett's perception in a completely different mirror. The proof of this is the fact that his principles were those underlying the peace agreement with Egypt and Jordan, the recognition of the PLO, the Oslo Accords, and the current political process to settle the historic conflict with the Palestinians. Despite his retirement from political life and his civic endeavors while he was still at the peak of his powers, his personality, work, and legacy left a deep imprint on political life and on society in the pre-state era and in the many years that have passed since the founding of the State of Israel. History has accorded Sharett the place he deserves in the pantheon of the greats of the nation, and his contribution to the shaping of the course of events that led to the state's founding and the people's rebirth will not be forgotten.

Dov Hoz

Dov Hoz was a princely and captivating figure with many contacts among members of Labor and other British parties. He may be counted alongside Chaim Weizmann, David Ben-Gurion, Chaim Arlosoroff, Ossishkin, Moshe Sharett, Zeev Jabotinsky, Nahum Sokolow, Kaplansky and David Hacohen as one to whom the world's great personages opened their doors.

I can provide a clue to Dov's noble character and warm personality by recalling his reaction when the blue-gray Willis automobile he had lent me got stuck in the sand of Emek Hefer after I had driven to the Kfar Vitkin beach to aid disembarkation of a group of illegal immigrants. Heart aflutter, I expected a rebuke or a scolding when I told him about the mishap and about my leaving the car there in the sand. But he surprised me with his winning smile, patted me on the shoulder, and was understanding, in view of the fact that I was a new driver at that time.

No less than he abhorred pretentiousness, boastfulness, and pontification, he disliked false modesty, and he would respond to such in conversation with characteristic subtle irony and good humor. For example, I heard him say more than once, "Listen, my friend, you're not big enough to make yourself that small." I've used that sentence myself on many occasions, never forgetting, of course, to attribute it to Dov.

Dov had a special talent for delivering harsh, direct criticism without causing pain or humiliation.

Dov was killed in 1940 in an automobile accident on the eve of a crucial trip to London, along with his wife Rivka, and a daughter, Tirza, and Yitzhak Ben Yaakov of Degania, a pioneer of Israeli aviation and manager of the Aviron Company. Dov's sister Hava was mortally wounded. Ironically, this fatal accident occurred when Dov was driving back from a visit with the "forty-three," whom he had come to visit before his trip to London. The only surviving member of his family is his daughter Tami (Tamar), who is married to Major General (Res.) Musik Gidron. Dov's death was a tragic blow, not only to his family, but to the whole nation. His death along with the untimely death of Eliyahu Golomb in 1945 left a vacuum that was especially felt in the times of distress and crisis the nation would later face. Their deaths afflicted me personally with a profound sadness.

Shaul Avigur

Shaul was a fascinating and exceptional person, wrapped in an aura of mystery. His personality represented the image of a revolutionary and a member of the underground, as rendered in the Russian literature of the era of the tsars. By nature he preferred to stay out of the limelight, completely avoiding public exposure and hiding behind a screen of secrecy with the few social contacts he had. Still he was determined, authoritative, and dominant vis-à-vis people and functionaries that worked with him, and as demanding and harsh on himself as he was on others. He rarely praised those under his command when a mission was successful, yet he would let others know in what high esteem he held them. And though he had some strange idiosyncrasies, they paled in comparison to the totality of his mythic personality. His lifestyle was Spartan in the extreme, both when he was in Israel and during his many years in Europe.

Shaul was one of the originators of Aliya Bet and he headed the organization from its inception, forming a cadre of talented workers and helpers both within and outside the kibbutz movement.

His original surname was Meirov, but after his seventeen-year-old son, Gur, was killed in the War of Independence, he adopted the surname Avigur, meaning "the father of Gur." The loss of his only son had a profound effect upon him, and he bore his tragedy with supreme heroism. He even missed his son's funeral since the War of Independence was raging and his services were needed to coordinate the procurement and shipment of arms from Europe. Only after the first truce came into force did he ask Ben-Gurion to relieve him to return to Israel and stay with his family at Kibbutz Kinneret.

Gur Meirov had stayed with his father in Tel Aviv for extended periods during his childhood. He was an enchanting child, smart, ebullient, and fearless—a trait characteristic of youngsters in the kibbutz movement, moshavim, and other agricultural populations. He used to love it when I gave him rides on my motorcycle through the city streets whenever I visited Shaul's flat. Only someone who had seen the transformation in Shaul's personality when he would play with Gur could possibly know what real *joie de vivre* is. It was hard to tell who was more gleeful, the father or the son. Gur's mother, Sarah, used to visit often with my wife in our Tel Aviv flat, and her visits became even more frequent during the years I spent in prison. On Shaul's frequent trips to Jerusalem, he would invite my wife to go along with him, hoping she would obtain a visitor's permit to the prison.

Shaul could never be drawn into small talk and always insisted on sticking to the subject at hand. There are any number of stories, with a substantial kernel of truth, about his habit of suddenly cutting off the person he was speaking to with a sudden "Goodbye" the moment the topic of conversation had been covered to his satisfaction, leaving the other person dumbstruck. To divert him from the projects that he was involved in for anything resembling recreation was impossible, even during his extended stays abroad. Once, and once only, Ehud Avriel managed to trick him into going to the Folies-Bergère Theater in Paris, but Shaul was so shocked by the semi-clothed dancers that he resolved to never again be tempted by such coaxing. He even considered meeting for a meal at a restaurant an unacceptable indulgence.

When I first started working with Avigur in 1933, he would search my desk drawers to make sure I had not left any documents or papers of any kind. Once, when he found such a document, he reprimanded me so strongly that his scolding haunted me for years.

People whose work brought them in contact with him were in awe of his unique personality, but no amount of effort could succeed in penetrating his personal armor, and few could form close personal relationships with him beyond the strictly formal contacts. He had a tendency to categorize people based on information about them that had nothing to do with their direct assignments. At the same time, to those few who did manage to find their way into his heart and win his confidence, he gave his unstinting trust.

He greatly admired, and was influenced by, Berl Katzenelson, who he met with often at his office at the *Davar* newspaper and at our office at the Executive House of the Histadrut. Shaul was one of the chosen few who had any influence on Ben-Gurion. He even played a key role in the attempts to settle the Lavon crisis, in whose wake Ben-Gurion resigned from Mapai and founded a new party, Rafi.

Even after the War of Independence, when I left the defense establishment and worked privately, Shaul used to phone me at all hours—sometimes five or six in the morning—to recruit me for various voluntary missions. All the workers used to complain bitterly about this habit of inviting people to meetings at the earliest possible hour, and they applied all their resourcefulness to urge him to postpone the meetings until a later hour. His early-bird nature probably resulted from his having lived on the Kibbutz where he would set out to work in the field at dawn. When I first started working with him, I would try to get to the office before dawn—in order to be there before him, a hopeless undertaking that only disturbed my wife's rest.

Shaul was responsible for founding and heading the secret organization "The Liaison Office" (later called "Nativ") which he also headed. This body's mission was to establish contacts with Jews behind the Iron Curtain, especially in the Soviet Union, and supply them with educational material about Israel. The Liaison Office also brought Jews from Eastern Europe to Israel, if only a small number, in accordance with the restrictions of that period.

One of Avigur's close assistants in this undertaking was Aryeh "Lova" Eliav, who worked under the guise of second secretary at the Israeli embassy in Moscow and secretly distributed a great deal of educational material.

Eliav combed the length and breadth of the Soviet Union countless times in an effort to make contact with its Jewish communities, but he was forced to return to Israel after the KGB picked up his trail and began to harass him.

Avigur's personal and moral stance carried a great deal of weight among the leadership of Mapai. In matters of security and in the areas of clandestine activity, the country's leaders considered him an expert and the primary authority. He was privileged to have some influence on Ben-Gurion and served as his aide in the Defense Ministry until the mid-1950s. In addition, by virtue of his personal qualities and his exacting moral and ideological code, he was viewed as the conscience of Mapai, and he headed numerous committees investigating affairs that shook the party and the Israeli Political Institution.

Shaul Avigur suffered for many years from a rare and incurable disease that caused attacks of irritation and swelling on his face and all over his body. But no suffering kept him from carrying on with his work, from dawn until very late at night. In all the years I worked with him, I don't remember him ever taking a vacation, even for a day. When he had severe attacks of his disease, he would work in his flat in Tel Aviv. He would sit in his bed and talk with one worker after another, in an endless procession. He would also work at home during the hot summer months, with no air conditioning, naked from the waist up. Inspired by Avigur's dedication, I even returned to the office the day after my wedding. When business brought me to the home of Eliyahu Golomb, his wife, Ada, and Golda Meir met me there. Eliyahu claimed that life in the underground had become second nature to me, as proven by the fact that even my marriage to Tania was a clandestine affair. He waved my apologetics aside, and claimed that even at a time full of calamities and bloody riots, normal life must go on. This was in 1936, the first year of the riots, when Jews fell at the hands of Arab murderers daily.

Shaul used to drink one glass of tea after another, and when he was in a good mood, he would offer a glass to his guest. A glass of tea had a soothing effect on him; it cheered him up, and suddenly he would become sociable. He would even show his sense of humor, accompanied by outbursts of laughter at his own jokes.

The concepts of "accumulated vacation days" or any other kind of benefits were foreign to us, and when I retired from the defense establishment in 1950, it never occurred to me that I might be entitled to compensation or to a pension with any kind of benefits for my seventeen years of service. An increment was also a concept foreign to Shaul, and if an employee got a raise, it was mostly to compensate for an increase in the size of his family.

Shaul's character was molded of values and conscience. Within the Labor movement, he was outstanding in his sense of duty to the service of the country and he had an impact on the shaping of the nature and worldview of his colleagues. The differences between him and some of those who worked under him arose from his character and his extreme caution in making operational decisions, as well as the exacting standards to which he held people. There is no doubt that among the leaders of that period, he stood out in his tremendous influence on the chosen few of his peers.

Eliyahu Golomb

It is impossible to discuss the molding of the pre-state political, military, and historical events without highlighting the central role that was played by Eliyahu Golomb. In the years preceding the establishment of the state until his death in 1945, he was the source of inspiration for many of the Haganah and the organized Yishuv's plans. The very pulse of the military and political activity could be felt in his home. Among the plans made there was the establishment and settlement of Hanita, under the leadership of Shaul Avigur, Yitzhak Sadeh, Yosef Avidar (Rochel), and Zvi Ben Yaakov. The site's assigned commander, Berger, representing the Haganah man in Jerusalem, was killed in one of the attacks by Arab bands, which were practically nightly occurrences. The "Tower and Stockade" settlements, which served as the advance guard in the struggle against the White Paper and later influenced the establishment of the new state's borders, were planned and directed by Shlomo Gur (Grazovsky) in Golomb's home. Here, too, the Palmach's operations to sabotage the Mandatory government and the British army's infrastructure were initiated. "The Night of the Bridges" and the destruction of the radar installations on Mount Carmel as well as the capture of the camp at Atlit and the liberation of the immigrants held there were planned in his home. The daring procurement missions and the break-in to capture the weapons at the British army Officers' School on the Carmel on Christmas Eve, carried out under the command of Yehuda Arazi, were also directed from his house.

Eliyahu Golomb's modest and cozy home was the hub for his family, but it was no less a meeting place and clubhouse for all the leaders and central figures of the Yishuv, the Haganah, and the settlement movement: Moshe Sharett, Yitzhak Ben-Zvi, David Hacohen, Golda Meir, Yosef Sprintzak, Shaul Avigur, David Remez, to name but a few. One of the more unusual visitors to Golomb's home was Binyamin Lubotzky (who would later change his name to Binyamin Eliav), at that time one of the leaders of the Revisionist Party. He served as liaison between Eliyahu and the Lehi and Etzel underground organizations, in an effort to limit, as much as possible, the violent nature of some of their missions. The high point of this coordination was the formation of the armed struggle movement (Tenuat Hameri), which served as the overall framework for the coordination of the activities of the various underground movements. Its joint command was headed by Yitzhak Sadeh, with the Haganah represented by Moshe Sneh and Yisrael Galili, and Etzel, to the best of my recollection, by its commander, Menahem Begin. This arrangement was preceded by a number of meetings between Eliyahu Golomb and Menahem Begin, which laid the foundations for this joint effort.

Frequent guests in the Golomb home were Ben-Gurion, Katzenelson and Beilinson. I think I remember seeing Mania and

Yisrael Shohat there as well. The Shohats were founders and leaders of the Hashomer organization in the 1920s.

Each guest was, always, warmly welcomed by Ada, Golomb's wife, who, despite the numerous distractions and bustle, was able to engage in pleasant conversation. Sharett's mother, who lived with the Golombs, also greeted guests. She was an individual brimming with wisdom, charm, and warmth in her own right, who enchanted and amazed everyone with the sharpness of her memory despite her advanced age. I remember when my oldest daughter, whom we named Dafna, was born (this was before Kibbutz Dafna was founded, and that name then was still very uncommon), she asked what the baby's name was, and when my wife started to answer, she cut her off with a movement of her hand and recalled the baby's name by heart.

In my wife's visits in Golomb's home, she became very friendly with him, his wife Ada, and the other members of the family. When I was in prison, her visits became more frequent. Once, afraid her visits might be burdensome to the family, she apologized to Ada, but Ada smiled and said there were so many "nudniks" who came to visit them that she couldn't even hope to compete. She added that they loved having her, that Eliyahu was very fond of her, and that he was always happy when she came.

Eliyahu Golomb's home was the birthplace of the Massada Plan, a plan that fortunately never had to be implemented. It was at the critical juncture of the Second World War in the Middle East, when the German army's Afrika Korps, under the command of General Rommel, broke through all of Britain's defensive lines in the western desert in 1942 and got as far as El Alamein, deep inside Egypt. The British had already begun planning a general retreat from Egypt and Palestine, as far as a planned line of defense in Iraq. According to our assessments, upon receiving reinforcements and building up its strength, the Afrika Korps would attack in an effort to conquer

Egypt and reach Alexandria, from where they would then conquer the Land of Israel. The feeling was that if Rommel managed to break through the front line at El Alamein, we would be faced with a very real danger of physical annihilation. The Massada Plan and plans for guerrilla warfare to be waged by Palmach companies trained by British officers in Mishmar Ha'Emek were prepared in case this worst-case scenario should materialize.

One of Golomb's striking qualities was that he made people feel very comfortable with him, that he could, by simply touching someone's arm, project his own tranquility on to the person speaking with him who might be anxious or overwrought. I remember well this movement that was quite typical of him. He used to enjoy testing Avigur's sense of humor—a great challenge, in view of Shaul's reputation of being a man without a sense of humor, because of his serious, scowling appearance.

The Golomb's home was run modestly and frugally. Every evening Ada would ask, "Eliyahu, when can we go to Tnuva to buy some provisions?" My wife Tania and I often stayed over at Ada and Eliyahu's house. One day their son David, called "Dodik," then eight or nine years old, came home with us to visit. As we were getting out of the car, the door closed on his hand. The excruciating pain he was in was obvious yet he bore the pain bravely, with no complaints and no tears. I remember my wife commenting that the apple didn't fall far from the tree.

I became an expert at finding Golomb when he was needed, which was no simple task as it was his custom not to let anyone know where he was going to be. Most often I would find him at the Fiat garage, where he would take his car for repairs and maintenance. I would see him standing next to his car, watching fascinated as they repaired the engine. He had a weakness for this pastime, and we had an agreement that I wouldn't let anyone know where I found him. And when people asked me where he was, I wouldn't say a word, indicating that this was top secret information.

The author's wife

Two Luminaries

Yitzhak Sadeh died in the early 1950s. I used to visit him often in his home on the Jaffa shore as he lay ill, as did many other friends: Palmach veterans, IDF officers, Haganah old-timers, the two men who served as head of the Haganah—Moshe Sneh and Israel Galili—and others. As Sadeh's condition worsened, his friends' visits became more frequent.

One day Galili phoned me to tell me that Yitzhak had asked me to come and see him. This was a few days before his death, which everyone knew was approaching. When I arrived, I found Israel Galili, Yigal Allon, Moshe Sneh, Nahum Sarig, Yosefle Tabenkin, and others already at his house. When I entered, Galili warned me not to mention politics, but to concentrate as much as possible on economic issues.

As I entered Yitzhak's room I realized that his days, and perhaps even his hours, were numbered. He was lucid and alert, but he was no longer the quarryman, whose body radiated health and power, and who could pack away half a kilo of meat during lunch at the Shtorch Restaurant, that we had known for so many years. His peace of mind and his acceptance of death, which was already casting its shadow over him, made a profound impression on me.

I pondered deeply, and I found myself hoping that when my time comes, I'll have the strength to cope with death with the same steadfast and serene spirit shown by Yitzhak Sadeh.

He died two days after I visited him.

In the 1950s, near Ma'ayan Harod, there was a gathering of many ex-Palmachniks, veterans of battles, who had retired from the army at the end of the war. Among the participants were Yigal Allon, Uri Brenner (deputy commander of the Palmach), Yigal Yadin (who had by then already retired as Chief of General Staff), Israel Galili, and Palmach brigade commanders in the War of Independence—Nahum Sarig, Yosefle Tabenkin, Mula Cohen, Yitzhak Rabin, Uri Yoffe, Shimon Avidan, and others. Many of the participants had made their mark on history at the time of the Arab revolt, and played key roles in the battles for the establishment of the state, as well as in later wars, in their roles as Chiefs of General Staff, heads of the Northern, Southern, and Central Commands, generals of the General Staff, Division Commanders, and other senior roles.

Yigal Allon made a speech to lift the spirits of the Palmach fighters who were still bitter following the disbandment of the Palmach. The words spoken then by Yigal, who was a brilliant, commander, the most outstanding in the War of Independence, reflected a man who was a born national leader. He stood out among his contemporaries in his gifts and merits: he had been blessed with a far-ranging, sweeping vision of our geo-strategic position in the region; a penetrating analytical ability; a social and national worldview that embraced all sectors; a deep conviction that a basis for co-existence with the Arab peoples could be found; a gentlemanly, noble personal image in his relations with friends as well as opponents; and the power of his belief in the correctness of his path and in his ability to convey that belief to the masses. His manner of speaking and his articulateness were manifestations of how Israeli he was to the core and gained him a place in the hearts of many fans and admirers. Especially winning were the charm and vigor that he radiated as he spoke.

After the Six Day War, Allon was the only Israeli leader who formulated and expressed a plan for the solution of the Israeli-Palestinian dispute, based on a separation of the two populations, and he even outlined the parameters for the solution. This fact, more than any other, testifies to his visionary political worldview and to the potential and promise that he embodied as a leader and a statesman. All this in addition to his being a military thinker, who drew many of his ideas from the British Captain Liddle-Hart, strategist and acclaimed teacher of the theory of military tactics. He adopted the strategic and tactical principles of outflanking and an indirect approach from Liddle-Hart's theory; these principles were to become part of the Palmach's and the IDF's doctrine of combat (Liddle-Hart had nothing but praise for our commanders' application of his teachings during the War of Independence and the Six Day War).

The political plan that bears his name, the Allon Plan, which he formulated right after the Six Day War, remains, to this day, the formula and basis from which the various solutions to the dispute that have been put forward are derived. He formed a special relationship with the Israeli Arabs, especially the Arabs of the Galilee. Every year he arranged a festive get-together for representatives of the Arab settlements with his many Jewish friends from all over the country. In approaching a solution to the Israeli-Palestinian conflict, Allon considered the Israeli Arabs a basic building block, serving as a sort of experimental laboratory for Jewish-Arab coexistence.

I learned about the important contribution Allon's studies in England had made to the development and expansion of his education at a lunch meeting with Allon and the editor-in-chief of the leading Norwegian newspaper, *Dage Blat*. Lunch was at Jerusalem's Mandarin Restaurant where Allon liked to invite his guests. When I arrived at the restaurant, I found the Norwegian editor already sitting at our table. I joined him, and we both waited for Allon. He came at the appointed hour and asked how we were, but instead of sitting with us he went into the kitchen, the waiters at his heels. Seeing the Norwegian's wonderment at Allon's behavior, I suggested that we both go take a look at what was going on in the kitchen. The editor was amazed at what he saw—Allon shaking the hand of every one of the kitchen workers, each of whose names he knew, asking how the family was, and then repeating this performance with each of the waiters. I had seen Allon do this on previous occasions, but the Norwegian editor was dumfounded by this display and whispered to me that he had never seen this in his journalistic career and in the many meetings he had had with a wide variety of world personalities and leaders. I can testify to the fact that this ritual was not for the benefit of this particular guest, but was repeated whenever he happened to be in that restaurant.

In conversation with his guest, Allon spoke about the social and economic issues the state had to cope with. He spoke a rich, fluent English, on a par with highly educated English university graduates. The editor was very impressed by Allon's lecture and said so at the end of the meal. I too was surprised by Allon's erudition and his analysis of these issues.

I once happened to be present when Allon was dealing with a crisis; this happened in his office at El Al House in Tel Aviv, in 1970 when he was serving as minister of education and deputy prime minister. As we spoke, he got a phone call from the United States. On the other end of the line, Prime Minister Golda Meir told him that the top American leadership was very concerned for the regime of King Hussein after the Syrian army had invaded northern Jordan. The two of them agreed that the IDF would move armored forces in broad daylight to carry out military maneuvers as a warning to the Syrian heads of government.

He immediately summoned the minister of defense to bring him up-to-date on the development and to decide on a plan of action with him. At the same time, he phoned the government secretary, instructing him to call a meeting of the government for its approval of these steps. As it turned out, the Syrian army retreated from northern Jordan in response to the IDF's actions and King Hussein's regime was saved. During all this, Yigal Allon remained composed, exercising his authority as acting prime minister with wisdom, restraint, and moderation.

I can't help expressing my conviction that, were Yigal Allon still with us today, the course of the country's history would have taken a different turn. He would have been elected to lead the Labor Party and would have been its candidate for prime minister, to steer the ship of state to safety. I realize that history does not recognize the words "if only" and deals not in speculation but facts. However, since I don't pretend to be a professional historian, I take the liberty to adhere to what I believe, to give wings to my imagination and my intuition, and to conjecture that things might have turned out in accordance with my prediction.

At the initiative of Allon, another smaller gathering of ex-Palmachniks took place in 1972 at the Ginossar Guest House to mark David "Dado" Elazar's promotion to Chief of General Staff after Haim Bar-Lev. Speeches were made at this gathering by Allon, Benny Marshak, Haim Bar-Lev, Dado, and also Uri Brenner, if I'm not mistaken. It was a memorable party, particularly since many of the guests hadn't seen one another for many years.

I was also invited and came with my wife, who was the secretary of the Field Companies' first training course for squad commanders, held in 1939 at Kfar Giladi, under the command of Eliyahu Cohen (later Major General Ben-Hur). Allon used to drop in on the course, so that as early as 1939 my wife got to know him and to admire his radiant personality.

At an event marking the change-over of chiefs-of-staff on February 2, 1972.
Seen here—from left to right—the incoming chief-of-staff, David Eleazar,
and his wife Telma; Minister Yisrael Galili; Ruth Allon; Yigal Allon, the
outgoing chief-of-staff; Haim Bar-Lev and his wife; the author

Benjamin (Benny) Marshak, one of the Palmach commanders,
speaks at the party to mark the change-over of chiefs-of-staff.
In the background, the author and his wife

The author and his wife at a meeting with Yigal Allon, deputy prime minister. At the party to mark the change-over of chiefs-of-staff, Haim Bar-Lev and David Eleazar (Dado). February 2, 1972

Deploying for a Possible German Invasion

During World War II, members of the Palmach participated in the first assault by the British and Australian forces in Lebanon. Among them were Yigal Allon and Moshe Dayan. Dayan lost an eye in one of the battles of that campaign. The British army was helped also by the Palmach's undercover unit, *Mista'aravim*, manned, among others, by Israel Ben-Yehuda (Abdu), Haim Levakov, Yosef Fein from Degania, Yehoshua (Josh) Palmon, Tuvia Arazi, and Yeruham Cohen (the "Gingy", later to become Yigal Allon's adjutant), who had spent time in Lebanon and Syria on intelligence gathering and other missions long before Britain's invasion of those countries. Tuvia Arazi was arrested in Beirut by the Lebanese secret police, sentenced to many years' imprisonment, and broke his leg in an escape attempt. Eventually, Yosef Fein, with the help of his many contacts in Lebanon, managed to rescue him and return him to Palestine.

In the early years of the war in the Middle East, David Hacohen was the central figure in the network of ties between the political department of the Jewish Agency and the Haganah High Command with British military intelligence in the region. Yitzhak Sadeh, appointed by Haganah head Moshe Sneh, Eliyahu Golomb, and Haganah headquarters to take charge of the Massada Plan, worked together with Yigal Allon and Hacohen to organize training in sabotage and guerilla warfare. The courses were conducted in a school located in Mishmar Ha'Emek, and Palmach companies trained there, led by British officers under the command of Major Hammond (a lecturer in history at a prestigious university in England). Sadeh and Allon commanded those companies, assisted by Meir Giron, who administered the finances and worked out the logistics, and by Aharon Leshem (Lashevsky), Sadeh's organizational and managerial assistant.

With the defeat of the British Eighth army under the command of Generals Wavell, Auchinleck, Richie, and Cunningham in battles against Rommel's Afrika Korps in the western desert, the Yishuv's political and security horizon darkened ominously. Anxiety gripped the Yishuv in the face of what could be expected if Rommel succeeded in breaking through the last line of defense at El Alamein.

The British began intensive preparations to retreat to a line of defense that they had established in Iraq. In view of this bleak outlook, the cooperation between the Haganah and British Military Intelligence grew. This cooperation was based on a plan to train Land-of-Israel forces to hound the German army—to sabotage bridges, roads, communications, and other strategic objectives. As part of the same framework, a plan was made to fortify, arm, and prepare the Carmel mountain range to serve as a kind of "Massada," should the situation become apocalyptic. In light of this most dire of all possible pictures, the top ranks of the Haganah convened with their senior officers and the Palmach units in Mishmar Ha'emek. The designated meeting place was the forest that had been planted on the hill overlooking the settlement.

I drove to this conference with Eliyahu Golomb, and I clearly remember his attempt to get to the hill by car, despite my warnings and those of other passengers that the area was full of rocks, and impassable by car. Characteristically, he tried to deal with this "challenge," until in the end the car got stuck on one of the rocks, its rear wheels up in the air. It required the combined efforts of an entire platoon to lift the car and place it back on the ground.

Participants in the conference were Golomb, Moshe Sneh, Yitzhak Sadeh, Yigal Allon, and Israel Galili. Sneh, who had recently arrived from Poland and had been appointed head of the Haganah, passed his "trial by fire" by appearing at this conference. He was a new and unknown figure, but the sober, impressive speech he made won the hearts and the admiration of the participants. He analyzed the dangers facing Jewish settlement from the Arabs in Palestine and the neighboring states on the one hand and from the possible conquest of the land by the German Afrika Corps on the other. In a wide-ranging analysis, he surveyed the many daunting threats and dangers, while at the same time projecting confidence and conveying the urgent need for the Yishuv to prepare itself in every way possible to cope with the existential dangers facing it.

The speeches of Sneh, Golomb, Galili, and Sadeh detailed the background of our cooperation with British Military Intelligence and explained the decision to cooperate with them even more closely simultaneously with our political struggle against the prohibitions of the White Paper and the mandatory government, in the spirit of Ben-Gurion's formula: "We will fight against Hitler as if there were no White Paper, and we will fight against the edicts of the British government as if there were no war against Hitler." It is true that Ben-Gurion was not present on that particular occasion, but his spirit and vision were felt very strongly.

It was Yigal Allon who was the most concrete and purposeful of all. He suggested that if the British did indeed pull out, the Palmach would need an enormous quantity of explosives to destroy the bridges at the country's borders. In the spirit of the friendship and comradeship that we two felt for each other, he complained to me that the explosives the Haganah High Command had allotted to him were insufficient. In accordance with his request, I obtained another two hundred fifty kilograms of explosives of the type called Ten, manufactured by Ta'as.

Procurement of the Ships
Nora and Shayo for Arms Shipping

During my stay in Italy in November 1947 to organize the arms shipment, as told in the previous chapter, I worked with Yosef "Yoske" Yariv. Before I left Italy with the documents for the big shipment, we spoke about the future of our activities, and I advised him of a man named Efraim Ilin, whom I had met in prison, where he was being interrogated by the British secret police regarding his membership and involvement in Etzel and Lehi operations. I described him as a resourceful businessman, who, after World War II, had transferred his business activity to Italy, where he had developed and expanded it diligently. He was engaged in the import of cotton from Egypt and textile manufacturing and marketing in Italy, whose fashion-conscious people had emerged from the war practically in rags. I advised Yoske that, in times of trouble, he would do well to turn to Ilin with his extensive connections in business and social circles in Italy.

I made a similar suggestion to Meir Giron, David Hacohen's trusted assistant, before he left for Italy in the period that preceded our War of Independence to coordinate finances for arms procurement and for Aliya Bet in Italy, under Pino Ginsburg, treasurer for arms procurement and clandestine immigration. Aharon Weisberg of Solel Boneh also recommended him to Ilin, who knew him and was impressed by his commercial activity in Italy.

Our arms procurement people in Italy invested a great deal of effort in the search for a ship to transfer arms purchased by us in Czechoslovakia and then sent by rail to the port in Sibenik (near Split) in Yugoslavia, but these efforts were in vain. Ehud Avriel, whom Ben-Gurion pressed to expedite the arms shipment, concluded that salvation would not come from the procurement people. He sent Hanan Guy and Levy Argov (Kopelevich), two of his aides in Czechoslovakia, to Italy to procure a ship. They met with Yosef Yariv and Meir Giron in Italy and explained our problem.

To acquire and load a ship and send it on its way from a port in Italy were extremely complex actions, involving complicated procedures and an abundance of paperwork. A formal legal procedure existed for the purchase and registration of the ship. Herein lay the key to the success of the mission, for the transfer of ownership might arouse the suspicion of the Italian authorities regarding the legality of the purpose for which the ship was being bought. But even if we overcame this obstacle, there were many other things that still had to be done, such as insuring the cargo, preparing bills of lading, the manifest, and so on. The arms procurement people lacked the technical and professional knowledge to carry out such a complex job.

Yoske Yariv and Meir Giron remembered what I had told them about Efraim Ilin's business and commercial know-how. They told Hanan Guy and Levi Argov about him and arranged a meeting between them that resulted in their cooperative effort and the purchase of a ship.

Hanan Guy's area of specialization in the Institute for Clandestine Immigration was shipping deals and purchase of vessels; therefore, Ehud Avriel appointed him to coordinate this mission and Levi Argov to assist him. Meir Giron and Yosef Yariv joined them, and the four set about planning the purchase of the ship. Ilin himself had never engaged in this type of activity before and he came to the conclusion that he and Avriel's people would not be able to jump these hurdles on their own, and that they must rely on local professionals who would function as their "front" in negotiations for the purchase of the boat. He spoke with a friend and business associate by the name of Francesco Parizzi, scion of one of the aristocratic families in the region, who enjoyed a position of honor in Italian business circles and managed an Italian shipping agency, Adriatica, in Venice.

In a discussion with him, the purchase of a ship named *Nora*, anchored in the port at Bari and carrying a load of salt, was suggested. Parizzi began negotiations with the owners, the Greek Consul in Venice, and his partner. It was agreed that once the ship, with its cargo of salt, arrived in Venice, Hanan Guy and the others would examine it. If it was found fit and the price was right, the purchase would be made. The examinations showed the ship to be in good condition, and the price that had been negotiated also seemed reasonable. Ilin resolved the problem of ownership transfer when he managed to convince the owners to keep the ship registered formally in their name.

The cargo of arms would be covered by boards and concealed under a shipment of onions and potatoes bought in the city of Marano from a Jewish vegetable wholesaler named Wishkin. The ship had a 600-ton capacity, 200 tons of which were intended for the vegetables. During the ship's stop at the port in Venice, the salt remaining in the hold from its previous sailing was washed away. As the ship was being prepared to set sail, the customs police came for a random inspection. Two large transmitters, which were intended for use by the communications system in Palestine in times of emergency, were already aboard and aroused fears that they would be discovered in the course of the inspection. When Ilin saw the customs police approaching the ship, he gave instructions to toss the instruments into the sea, knowing that if they were discovered by the police, all that had been accomplished would be for naught. And in fact, the inspection went smoothly.

On the eve of sailing from Venice to Sibenik, the crew rebelled because they had a feeling that this voyage was a departure from the routine of lawful marine transport. The arms procurement representatives received word of the rebellion from Parizzi's people in Venice and they rushed to the ship, which was anchored at Venice's Lido shore. They assembled all the members of the crew, including the captain and the first officer, and Efraim Ilin made an impassioned speech to them in fluent Italian, in which he admitted that the ship was sailing to Palestine. With extreme pathos he argued that the Italian people had an obligation to extend their hands to the Jewish people, to assist them in their fateful struggle for the existence of their ancient homeland and in establishing a haven for the survivors of the Holocaust in Europe, who were returning to their homeland. At the end of his speech, he said that anyone who didn't want to make the trip was free to leave. The captain told Meir Giron and Ilin that Ilin's ardent speech had completely changed the crew's attitude, and it was his guess that no one was going to leave.

The ship set sail for the port of Sibenik, where the arms and the vegetables bought in Italy for concealment were loaded. On board the ship was Binyamin Yerushalmi, a key operative in the Institution for Clandestine Immigration, with a communications technician to maintain contact with Palestine in an emergency. Because of the slow passage of the ship and the radio silence it was careful to maintain, Shaul Avigur began to fear for its safety, but his fears proved groundless, and the ship arrived at the Tel Aviv port on time, on April 2, 1948. On hand to welcome her were Aharonchik Leshem (Lashevsky), in charge of arms procurement matters at the port; Hillel Dan, general manager of Solel Boneh; Pinik of Ruchama, who was in charge of arms procurement for the country; Yosef Yariv; Avraham Broshi of Kibbutz Shamir; and Yitzhak Weiman.

Due to the radio silence, there had been no contact with the ship, and the arms procurement team headed by Yosef Yariv kept watch from one of the rooftops, trying to spot it as it approached. When it came into sight, it was identified by Yoske Yariv, who had just arrived in Palestine with the documents of the shipment; Yoske was the only one of all the arms procurement team in Palestine who had seen the ship and could recognize it. After the unloading, the mission's operatives were invited to David Ben-Gurion's house, where they also met Eshkol, Sapir, and Galili, who praised them for the role they had played in the operation, so vital to the course of the war.

The weapons arrived at the various units still smeared with a layer of grease. Most of them were intended for Operation Nahshon, the operation to break the Arab siege around Jerusalem, and went to equip the escort unit of the convoy to Jerusalem commanded by Harry Yoffe.

At this point I feel an obligation to write a few words about this man. Harry Yoffe had made *aliya* (immigration to Israel) from South Africa, was among the first recruits from Palestine to the British army, and, with the rank of major, commanded an Israeli company in the Transport Corps. He proved his courage and devotion to his men when he went down with his company during a German air attack on the ship on which he and his company were sailing from Egypt to Greece. He saved many soldiers from drowning and was decorated by the British army for his conduct and for the bravery he showed in this tragedy.

Harry Yoffe's activities in the Haganah began during the riots of 1936, when I recruited him with his car to drive Shaul Avigur and other Haganah commanders for security and operational purposes. Private cars were a rarity in those days, and he showed a laudable willingness to place himself at our disposal, even taking his turn manning the Haganah Headquarters, which had to be staffed twenty-four hours a day.

Later, during the War of Independence, when the convoys to besieged Jerusalem started rolling, he commanded the large convoy that was eventually trapped at Sha'ar Hagai (Bab'el Wad) under heavy fire from a large Arab force. The convoy found itself in desperate straits. Ahead of it, Ben-Gurion was traveling to Jerusalem, but he managed to get through Sha'ar Hagai before the battle started. Yitzhak Rabin, commander of the Harel Brigade was also in that convoy. The situation was hopeless and verged on disaster, when Rabin managed to break through despite the heavy fire and to reach Kiryat Anavim, where he called for reinforcements from the men of his brigade. Subsequently, false and malicious rumors were spread that Rabin had attempted to escape from the battlefield, while in fact, he had performed a daring, perilous feat.

Harry Yoffe suffered a critical injury in Jerusalem in early May 1948, as he jumped from his car under fire and the handle of his gun hit his thigh and made a ghastly rip through his flesh. He languished, bedridden, for several years. His wife Yemima nursed him in their Rothschild Boulevard flat in Tel Aviv until he died of complications from his injury.

While the *Nora* was still en route from Sibenik to Palestine, another ship, the *Shayo*, with an eight hundred-ton capacity and the ability to hold even more cargo, was being loaded. This vessel was purchased by Ada Sereni and Yehuda Arazi. When the ship was anchored in the port of Venice, Efraim Ilin was assigned to find the additional appropriate staff to complete the crew, to load the camouflaging merchandise onto the ship, prepare the bills of lading and the manifest, and to see to the other details that the sailing entailed. Unfortunately, after the *Shayo* set sail, headed for the port at Dalmatia, agents of the British Security Service appeared in Venice and started questioning those who had been involved in the preparations for the sailing, including the agent, the food supplier, and the Francesco Parizzi Shipping Agency. When word of the investigation reached our people, the arms were unloaded immediately and the ship changed course for a different destination.

A few days before the declaration of the establishment of the state, the ship was reloaded with arms stored in Yugoslavia and that had originated in Czechoslovakia. As a result our people had to make every effort to help the crew to overcome their agitation when they realized the ship was headed toward a region at war.

The ship arrived in Israel a few days after the declaration of the state, and the vital cargo of arms that it brought meant reinforcements for the combat units engaged in bitter battles at several fronts against the invading armies. Later on, it was pressed into service to deliver fuel for the fifty Spitfire planes mentioned above.

Ilin was also the man who made contact with the manufacturer of the crashing boats and got the Israeli fleet to check the possibility of buying them and eventually used them in an attack on the Egyption fleet aiming to bomb Israel and downed the "Ibrahim-El-Awal", the flagship of Flotila and one of the accompanying corvettes.

The Levi Eshkol I Knew

In 1940, Levi Eshkol replaced Shaul Avigur as the person in charge of Ta'as as well as of arms acquisitions by the National High Command of the Haganah. In conjunction with these changes, Eshkol also "inherited" me as his assistant. As time passed, we developed a close relationship, and he would consult with me from time to time.

The first assignment he gave me was to buy him a car. Since it was the second year of World War II, this was no simple matter. The import of automobiles to Palestine had stopped at the outbreak of the war, and the British government required car owners to hold a special permit. Very few Jews had cars or licenses and those who did guarded them as their most precious possession and were not willing to part with them at any price. So, it was next to impossible for me to convince anyone to sell me his car despite my explanations as to whom it was for and how vital it was to sell it to the Haganah. I was finally able to get a car from Eli Kirschner, an attorney from South Africa, who had an almost new Mercury. I'll never forget his magnanimity in giving up his car with the license for Eshkol's use. That was no small sacrifice in those hard times.

Since Eshkol had never owned a car and didn't know how to

drive, one of my tasks was to teach him this skill. The driving lessons took place on the almost deserted roads of the Sharon. My wife Tania used to sit in the backseat during these lessons, and her heart would quiver whenever Eshkol was behind the wheel. He used to take the car to Kibbutz Degania on weekends, while during the rest of the week it was at my disposal for the work I had to do.

When World War ii ended and the import of automobiles to Palestine resumed, Eshkol exchanged the Mercury for a new Buick. One day I took the car from him at the Jewish Agency offices in Jerusalem—he was a member of its Executive—to carry out a job he had given me. As I was driving from Jerusalem to Tel Aviv, I realized, terrified and helpless, that the brakes were failing. This was at the descent from the Kastel, and the car was picking up speed. Luckily, the problem had become evident on the descent of the old road, hewn out of the mountainside, which wound serpentinely and adjoined the side of the mountain to my right. I realized that in this desperate situation the only way to stop the car was to brush against the side of the mountain. The strategy worked. Gradually the car slowed down and eventually came to a halt, its right side severely damaged and dented. An examination at the garage showed that because the brakes' oil pump was empty they had stopped working completely. People in the oncoming cars must have been astonished at the peculiar driver who was intentionally brushing against the mountainside. There's no knowing how this near accident might have ended if Eshkol himself had been driving. I hope I'm doing no discredit to his memory by saying that Eshkol was not exactly a virtuoso in the art of driving.

On the day of my sudden and unexpected release from prison in 1946, before even seeing my family, I visited Eshkol, who was then serving as secretary of the Tel Aviv Workers' Council. I arrived at Beit Brenner just as a meeting of the council was in progress. When he saw me, Eshkol froze in his chair, finding it hard to believe his eyes. But he quickly recovered and embraced me, while those at the meeting looked on, amazed at his strange performance. When he noticed this, he introduced me to all present and told them about our work together when he had served as a member of the Haganah National Command. Our friendship and our occasional meetings and conversations continued after he was appointed director general of the Ministry of Defense at the beginning of the War of Independence.

At one of our meetings in the early 1960s, when Eshkol was serving as prime minister and minister of defense, I found him disturbed and agitated, which wasn't like him. In answer to my question about the reason for his gloomy mood, he poured his heart out to me and told me about the difficulties placed in his way by his political opponents whenever he had to make policy decisions on matters of defense. His opponents' positions were not to be dismissed lightly, considering that they were held by some of the most senior retired leadership of the Ministry of Defense.

To illustrate the kind of obstacles set in his path, he told me about his plan to purchase 50 Skyhawk planes from the American weapons industry. His objective was to crack the traditional wall of resistance that the United States government was then putting up against supplying arms to Israel. The truth is that American policy did not leave the Israeli security system many options, since all our attempts at procurement from the American arms industry were shattered by the barrier of their opposition. But Eshkol's idea was a turning point in Defense Ministry policy, which had always seen France as the IDF's main arms supplier and as Israel's strategic and defense partner.

The result of that policy had been our exclusive dependence on the government of France for the supply of arms for the IDF's various needs. By having made ourselves completely dependent on France, Eshkol felt we were putting all our eggs in one basket, a situation which gave him no rest from the day he assumed the mantle of leadership. He deemed it necessary to change this situation and to do the political groundwork that would facilitate forming close ties with the United States as well, which, thus far had practiced an extreme opposition policy on the subject of Israel's security.

Of course, Eshkol knew that America's reluctance to provide Israel with weapons was the result of a global policy and a fear of the damage that would likely be caused to its relations with Arab nations. However, despite the slim chances of success, he was determined to set out on this course and enlist the backing of every sympathetic element in the American government and public. True, the Kennedy administration had supplied a number of Hawk anti-aircraft batteries to Israel in the early 1960s, an arrangement arrived at in a meeting between Kennedy and Ben-Gurion at the Waldorf-Astoria Hotel. But that had been a one-time deal, the "excuse" for which was that Hawk batteries were considered clearly defensive in nature.

As much as the purchase of the latest, most sophisticated American weapons was of great importance in and of itself, Eshkol primarily had his eye on its added value. His assumption was that as their provision of arms to Israel increased, so would America's commitment to Israel's security and political standing and its support for our position in the region.

The fact that the purchase of the Skyhawks from the United States was not intended to take the place of the fifty Mirage jets ordered from France did nothing to weaken the resistance of some of the Defense Ministry people, opponents of Eshkol, who preferred to pin all their hopes for acquisitions, security and strategic relations on France alone. Eshkol was well aware of the resistance to his initiative, of the criticism and the blame that would be directed at him for jeopardizing our close security relations with France. He was particularly wary of the reaction of the charismatic General Ezer Weismannn, who was considered the authority on everything involving air force equipment. Eshkol had to make a special effort to convince Weizmann to support his American move. At the same time, he was encouraged by the support he received from Chief of General Staff Yitzhak Rabin and from the Ministers Allon, Galili, and Pinhas Sapir, who were of one mind with him and backed him in strengthening Israeli relations with the Americans.

Everyone familiar with the prevailing circumstances at the time will recall how Eshkol moved mountains, avoided pitfalls, and overcame every obstacle in the way of establishing a broad-based infrastructure to form close ties and achieve cooperation with the United States in the areas of strategy and security. The aim was to gradually transfer the center of gravity of arms supplies to the IDF to American sources. This development eventually led to a reversal in Israel-United States relations, and the United States became our primary purveyor of arms and our political and security support in the region.

It takes no great amount of imagination to envision how help-less Israel would have been in the wake of the Six Day War, after De Gaulle and the French government imposed their arms embargo, if Eshkol hadn't broken the Americans' resistance. Ironically, France went so far as to violate her contractual commitment and cancelled the shipment of the fifty Mirage jets. Even the missile ships built in France for Israel were not delivered and were only recovered by the Israeli navy in the daring and clandestine Operation Cherbourg in December 1969.

There can be no doubt that without this dramatic about-face, which came about thanks to Eshkol's foresight, wisdom, common sense, and political instincts, Israel would have encountered dangers to its very existence. As it happened, the deeper American involvement in military aid to Israel became, the greater was Israel's weight in the strategic balance of the United States in the region, and the two parallel processes nourished each other.

Unfortunately, Eshkol's prodigious achievements and successes as minister of defense did not prevent his being dismissed from that office on the eve of the Six Day War, and all because he stammered in a speech he delivered over the radio—a slip which was blown out of proportion by his opponents and caused an uproar. Historical perspective shows how bizarre and groundless this incident was. Even his intention to transfer the defense portfolio to Yigal Allon, an accomplished commander who had proven his gift for military leadership in the War of Independence, was thwarted by a wave of propaganda and personal attacks, as well as the pressure applied by the Herut, Liberal, and Rafi parties to appoint Moshe Dayan, an appointment that they presented as a precondition to their joining the unity government.

Yigal Allon had already started working at the job, based on the decision of Alignment (Ma'arach) institutions, had studied the operational plans and had even toured several fronts and met with the heads of the various commands together with Eshkol. When he realized how much political agitation there was, he understood that his appointment was threatened, and he told me about it. I suggested that he speak with Menahem Begin and Yosef Sapir who were about to join the government as the leaders of the Herut and Liberal Parties, and try to convince them to withdraw their opposition. He agreed. I volunteered to invite them through the offices of Yosef "Yoske" Kremerman, a Herut leader and Begin intimate (for this I took advantage of my friendship with him), and my brother Israel Sacharov, who was a senior member of the Liberal Party and on close terms with Yosef Sapir.

Both Kremerman and my brother agreed to my request and said they would bring Begin and Yosef Sapir to a meeting with Yigal arranged for the same day at three o'clock at the Lilit Café on Mazeh Street in Tel Aviv. However, shortly before the meeting, Yigal phoned me and asked me to call it off, since at an emergency meeting of the Alignment institutions that morning, it had been decided to accept the demand that Dayan be named defense minister.

There is no concealing the fact that, as things turned out, the appointment of Moshe Dayan to the post of minister of defense contributed a great deal, as evidenced in the boost to the morale of the officers and soldiers thanks to the prestige and reputation he had earned in the Sinai Campaign. Furthermore, everyone remembered the reversal Dayan brought about in the esprit-de-corps, structure, and group bonding in the IDF, and the fighting spirit with which he imbued the different units when he was appointed chief of staff during the period of severe recession that beset the army in the first years after the War of Independence. I'm happy to add that Yigal Allon himself also spoke favorably of Moshe Dayan in two lectures at which I was present: the first, two days before the beginning of the Six Day War, and the second at its conclusion. Allon described Dayan as an asset to our defense capabilities, and wished him luck on assuming his new responsibility.

Eshkol and the Six Day War

Everyone knows an army can't be built in one month, or even in a year. The truth of the matter is, the IDF reached the peak of its physical and spiritual power in the years that Eshkol served as minister of defense after painstaking work that started as early as the underground movements—principally the Haganah, but also, to a lesser extent, Lehi and Etzel—during the British mandate. Still, there is no denying that in the years leading up to the Six Day War, the IDF made great strides in quantity as well as in quality.

Our speedy and overwhelming victory in the Six Day War was made possible first and foremost thanks to the doctrine formulated by the IDF and approved by the government headed by Eshkol. The army and its various subdivisions were built on the cornerstone of this strategic doctrine, which, especially on the ground and in the air, served as a basis for the tactics and training programs and determined policy for the purchase and the manufacture of weapons, according to a strict order of priorities. This doctrine's salient points were that the regional defense units, based on the agricultural and semi-urban settlements, were to see to day-to-day defense needs, while the greatest part of the army would be concentrated in the offensive divisions. These included a tactical air force capable of crushing assault and one of the most highly respected in the world. In addition, our large and superbly trained armored corps was able to tilt the balance more than almost any corps has ever done, in the history of armored war has ever seen. Assisting the armored forces were our indomitable mechanized and mobile infantry and our paratroop brigades, able to act with flexibility, in both small and large units, both in frontal combat and behind enemy lines, according to the shifting needs of combat. Side by side with the combat divisions, the IDF established an array of efficient and essential services, without which the combat divisions would never have been able to accomplish what they did.

The IDF was then a sophisticated war machine, which also included an intelligence branch that showed astounding familiarity with the systems and plans of the enemy (perhaps even more than their commanders knew). We can only comprehend how the IDF High Command brought the army to a state of perfection, as manifested on the battlefield, if we keep in mind the power embodied in the entirety of our military system. Obviously, the formation of an army is not the exclusive accomplishment of the minister of defense and the chief of general staff alone. Like every large social enterprise, it, too, should be seen as the collective accomplishment of many.

There is no doubt that the entire government, especially the Ministerial Committee for Defense Matters, headed by Levi Eshkol, had no illusions, foresaw the danger, and saw to it that the army had economic resources and political and public backing, despite the oppressive economic burden this placed on the population. It was the Ministerial Committee that approved the IDF's strategic doctrine, thus shaping the orientation that directed the building of the forces.

It is true that the IDF has been blessed with a staff of exceptionally high professional caliber, suffused with a highly developed sense of mission that is untainted by any of the negative concomitants of militarism. But without the assistance, support, public backing, and bestowal of resources and priority to security needs in the national budget by Eshkol and his government, our decisive military achievements in the field of battle could hardly have been achieved. This is not to minimize the accomplishments of the army's commanders or of the leadership of General Yitzhak Rabin, who had the wisdom, with his characteristic modesty, to make the correct and decisive use of the means that the Eshkol government put at his disposal.

The IDF commanders established an army able to call up its forces and get organized with amazing speed, and with no outside help defeated all the Arab armies arrayed against it at the same time. It is true that it was the IDF that started the war in order to gain the advantage of surprise, but this is to be seen as a preemptive strike, which we were forced to make when the armies of Egypt, Jordan, and Syria all united at our borders under one command, with the clear objective of a simultaneous attack against Israel.

It is worth noting that under threat of immediate attack, Israel enjoyed advantageous political conditions on the eve of the Six Day War as it never had before. This, too, is to be seen as the fruit of the policy shaped by Eshkol and his government. It is possible to conclude that Israel had to attack its enemies as soon as the Egyptians blocked the Straits of Tiran or to conjecture that political steps should perhaps have preceded the shooting to test whether war might be avoided or to prepare the political conditions for an unavoidable all-out war. But there can be no doubt that delaying the start of the war for the sake of political overtures, despite the fact that the troops had already been drafted, turned out to be a blessing, even if other leaders' appraisal of the chances of a political effort was at variance with this. This was perhaps the only time that Israel was not condemned by the UN Security Council and did not require a friendly power's veto. Neither was the Soviet demand that

Israel retreat after the war to the June 1967 borders accepted by the rest of the world, and we enjoyed the accord of different parts of the world and more widespread support than what we had in 1948 and in the Sinai Campaign.

In the Sinai Campaign, two powers, France and Britain, stood by us openly, but despite this fact, we found ourselves isolated and threatened in the international arena to such an extent that our government had to return all that it had conquered. We were left without getting any real guarantees against threats to our freedom of shipping in the Straits of Tiran or against the possibility that Egypt might renew the attack on us, and without managing to obtain international agreement to our use of the Suez Canal. Egypt's expulsion of the UN Emergency Force and the obstruction of the Straits of Eilat on the same day proved how unstable and insubstantial were the political achievements that followed the brilliant military victory in 1956.

Since I am well acquainted with the facts, I will take the liberty of saying that the tempest that raged over the defense portfolios being removed from the hands of Eshkol and Allon undermined the nation's morale and delayed the establishment of a broad-based emergency government. It is possible that this quandary, evident to anyone and everyone, even served as a source of encouragement to the enemy camp.

Thus, we must acknowledge that the historic truth must take into account not only our brilliant victory in the Six Day War but also the role played by Eshkol in forging the IDF's might. At the same time, one must consider the victory as a collective act, achieved under the leadership of a farsighted government, combined with the voluntarism of a people who knew what they were fighting for and were prepared to sacrifice the best of their sons to attain it. But no one will object if I say that, above all, the victory belonged to the soldiers of the IDF, from the lowliest private to the chief of general staff, who showed himself to be a master planner and a superb commander. No one could possibly think that this victory was the fruit of sudden inspiration or last-minute improvisation.

If we examine the profound, diligent groundwork accomplished by the Ministry of Defense under Eshkol over the course of years to build the IDF and prepare it for war, a clear picture of the crying injustice ultimately done to Eshkol emerges. The blame for this must be laid at the doorstep of certain segments of Israeli society, some party leaders, and even a few of his colleagues within the party, who wrenched the defense portfolio from his hands just as these historic achievements were about to come to fruition, allowing their fruits to be plucked by others on the field of battle. The Eshkol that emerged from the war was not the old Eshkol who was full of optimism, vitality, human warmth, and infectious humor. His political opponents had exacted a very heavy price from him, as had the fickleness and weakness of many of his friends. Eshkol's close friends and acquaintances saw the wrong done to him as being twofold. The softness and hesitancy that were popularly ascribed to Eshkol, and which supposedly bespoke weakness of character, were actually manifestations of his openness, and his humanity, his preference for agreed-upon solutions and for resolving disputes pleasantly instead of through confrontation, brawling, and coercion. Hidden within these characteristics was a tough core. In times of decision on critical and fateful matters, this inner toughness would burst out of its shell and find its full expression, and everyone who ever worked with him was well aware of the inner strength that he embodied.

The How and the When of the Plan to Produce ABC Kits

In one of my meetings with Eshkol while he was serving as prime minister and minister of defense and with Finance Minister Zeev Scherf, I informed them of a contact I had made with a German factory that manufactured gas masks and other means of protection against ABC (atomic, biological, and chemical) warfare. I added that I had managed to interest the management in supplying Israel with the know-how and technical assistance for setting up a similar plant in Israel. The impetus to take this step arose from my concern that the circumstances in our region were presenting Israel with a challenge: to find a solution to the danger of unconventional weapons being used against the IDF and the civilian population. Our intelligence and security people had learned a great deal about the acquisition by some of the Arab states (Syria, Iraq, and Egypt) of chemical and biological weapons. (It should be noted that Egypt used chemical weapons in its war against Yemen.) Therefore, I intended to take advantage of the contacts I had developed with several scientists and industrialists in Germany in order to check out this possibility.

Eshkol's immediate reaction was skeptical. He pointed out the tremendous financial burden entailed in producing and storing millions of masks for use in an emergency. Zeev Scherf, in contrast, was in favor of the plan. He suggested passing on the cost of the manufacture of the masks to the citizenry, allowing them to spread out the payments over a long period of time.

Eshkol considered the idea worthy of deeper investigation. In agreement with Scherf, he decided to bring up the plan for discussion in the cabinet meeting and at the same time to consult with the professionals, in order to learn more about all aspects of the project's ramifications.

I saw a need to create a lobby to advance the project and discussed it in depth with the prime minister's military secretary, Major General Israel Lior, and Moshe Kashti, the director-general of the Ministry of Defense, who was enthusiastic about the plan. It goes without saying that I had no problem enlisting the support of Golda Meir, Pinhas Sapir, Yigal Allon, and Israel Galili; in view of the importance of equipping the civilian population and the IDF with ABC kits, they promised to urge Eshkol to promote the plan and see it through to its implementation.

One of the central questions was whether one of the defense industries or a private entrepreneur should set up the factory. I recommended giving preference to private individuals, since I assumed that the German factory would prefer to cooperate with private entrepreneurs rather than with a government body.

In the course of the discussion, I mentioned the name of Shlomo Bograd as a candidate who had the know-how and professional experience to carry out the project. Bograd, who was then the owner of a plant in Zichron Ya'akov for the production of explosives, had worked with me for many years at Ta'as before the establishment of the state and during the War of Independence. From our work together, I came to appreciate his organizational and managerial ability. I pointed out his qualities: a gift for organization, management, and implementation, extensive knowledge about the handling of explosives and other sensitive materials, diligence, and leadership. Eshkol and Scherf reacted skeptically and unfavorably, though they didn't deny his personal and professional talents. I stood firm by my opinion, and Eshkol and Scherf suggested a way of getting around the obstacle: that I personally collaborate with Bograd on the project.

While the discussions were going on at the Defense Ministry, I also spoke with Bograd. He was very interested and wanted to undertake the implementation of the project. When I told him about Eshkol and Scherf's reservations and their suggestion that I be a partner in the project, he accepted the idea enthusiastically. After we clarified the fine points of our partnership, a lawyer prepared a contract which we were to sign at a meeting at the Lilit Café on Mazeh Street in Tel Aviv.

For reasons I am unable to explain even to myself to this day, at the last minute I couldn't bring myself to sign the contract, and I decided not to participate in the project, although it was certainly attractive and promising in terms of its financial possibilities. (I suppose something in me resisted earning money from doing business with the defense establishment. Through the years I turned down many offers, for some reason shrinking from dealing in arms, as some of my friends and senior IDF officers did after their retirement—despite the fact that I believe there is no iniquity, weakness, or stain—moral or ethical—in such a pursuit. Quite the contrary: While they were working for their livelihood, more than a few of these agents provided crucial services to the defense establishment and to the economy of the state). At the same time, I was aware of the danger that my leaving at that critical moment was likely to jeopardize the continuation of the project.

I reassured Bograd, who was shocked and whose eyes were brimming with tears, and suggested others to whom he could he turn as a partner in my stead, including the Koor Cooperation, a joint venture between two of the largest workers' unions in Israel.

He was in favor of the idea and contacted the Koor management, which showed great interest in the proposal. Within a short time the partnership between Shlomo Bograd and the Koor concern was formed, and they combined forces to implement the project.

The Shalon plant was established in Kiryat Gat and was able to supply the entire civilian population and the IDF with gas masks during the Gulf War.

The First Fighter Planes and the Airlift from Czechoslovakia

Introduction

On May 10, 1948, five days before the declaration of the establishment of the state, I returned to Palestine from the United States where I had been for several months on Haganah business. My mission had been to organize shipments of machinery and industrial equipment for the production of arms. The equipment was procured by a group of local volunteers headed by Phil Alpert, Eli Shalit, and others, including a few young Israelis who were working or studying in the United States at that time, and who had been recruited for this operation at its outset by Slavin when he was in the United States. Phil Alpert was an amazingly gifted engineer, American-born, who was educated at American universities and who worked as Slavin's right-hand man for machinery and equipment procurement. Thanks to his prudent nature and painstaking approach to his work, he was the greatest asset to the Ta'as delegation in the United States. Eli Shalit was from Palestine but educated in the United States, and he excelled in original, imaginative thinking in the area of commerce and in forming relationships with professional and technical people that aided the delegation.

However, from time to time he would get carried away, and it was necessary to rein him in.

Slavin started this undertaking in 1945 when he was sent to the United States by David Ben-Gurion. I was assigned to organize the off-loading of the equipment—camouflaged and labeled as machinery for textiles or for metal processing—that arrived at the ports in Palestine. I had to register the equipment and store it where it would be well hidden. This was immediately after my release from prison. These consignments of camouflaged equipment arrived in Palestine under import licenses I had managed to obtain from Solel Boneh and from our pioneering industrialists in Palestine—Zalman Yerushalmi, Sam Zacks, Klir of the Argaman plants, Shenkar, owner of the Lodzia textile plant; the Pliz factory in Holon, and others in whose plants most of the imported equipment and machinery were stored.

On a visit to the United States in 1945, Ben-Gurion along with Eliezer Kaplan organized a group of first rank Jewish leaders and businessmen. One of these businessmen, Max Livingstone, placed his New Haven factory at our disposal during the nighttime hours when nobody was there, and there we would pack up most of the equipment and machinery for arms production, as well as a quantity of weapons that Jewish American war veterans had collected for us, in preparation for their transfer to the ports. The list of these people was prepared in consultation with a man named Montor, then the top-ranking official in the executive of the Jewish Agency in the United States. He took an active part in the organization and operation of this body.

This group was formed by Ben-Gurion and Yaakov Dori, who headed the Haganah delegation in the United States, and it was deployed by Slavin and Dori for vital Haganah missions. The first gathering of this body, before whom Ben-Gurion and Kaplan spoke, took place in Sonneborn's home, which was thenceforth nicknamed the "Sonneborn Institute." Ben-Gurion made a speech there which could be called prophetic, under the circumstances. He spoke of the need for extensive, far-reaching preparedness to create the conditions and do the groundwork for a military struggle with the British and the establishment of a Jewish state. It should be noted that this meeting took place in 1945, when the "dream" and the struggle of the Zionist movement and the Yishuv were focused on bringing a mere 100,000 Jews to Palestine. It is hard to imagine any other Zionist leader conceiving of a goal so far-reaching and revolutionary to equal the vision of Ben-Gurion. Those assembled were thrilled at his words. Some said they felt history itself was enveloping them.

All those present agreed to help pay for the purchase of great quantities of equipment offered for sale by arms factories at the end of World War II, and to place at our disposal their extensive contacts with key figures in the Jewish community and in the American economy, particularly with well-known American industrialists.

I had to invest a concerted effort and apply a great deal of pressure to persuade Galili and Slavin to agree to my return to Palestine on the eve of the declaration of the founding of the state, so that I could take part in the battles to come. I recommended entrusting the continued management of the delegation to Phil Alpert, considering that the lion's share of our procurement program* had already been accomplished by the delegation during my tenure at its helm. Having determined that Alpert was capable of managing the delegation until the completion of its work, I suggested that he be placed in charge of all activities, so that sending a replacement for me from Palestine would not be necessary.

I was brought to Palestine from Paris, via Geneva, on a Dakota air-

---

* The delegation's "shopping list" included machinery, equipment, raw materials, instruments and other elements necessary for the manufacture of mortars, shells, sub-machine guns, "Dror" light machine guns, and raw materials for the production of both high and low explosive materials.

plane owned by a South African Jew, who had placed himself and his two Dakota planes at the disposal of the Provisional Government of Israel. These two aircraft represented Israel's sole aviation channel. The plane was sent specially from Palestine to Europe to fly Teddy Kollek, Colonel David Marcus, Colonel Forester (an American non-Jew, who played a central role in the American Communication Corps and served the Haganah as professional advisor to Yaakov Yanai, commander of the Communication Corps), and myself home, after all of us were detained in Europe on our way to Palestine. We were forced to rent a Beechcraft airplane to take us from Paris to Geneva after several days of nerve-racking waiting in Paris.

Active at that time in the French capital was the attorney, Shchupak, whom David Remez, the designated minister of transport in the provisional government, had sent there to conduct negotiations with the French government and with Air France concerning the operation of an air route from Paris to Palestine by a subsidiary of Air France. The negotiations proceeded at a snail's pace, and everyday Shchupak was given false promises that the airway would be opened. As it turned out, these promises were not kept, and we despaired of flying directly from Paris to Palestine. We failed in an attempt to fly from Nice to Cyprus with the British BOAC, when the pilot refused to fly us as holders of Palestinian passports in keeping with the BOAC regulations then in effect. We had planned to rent a motorboat in Cyprus in order to get to Haifa Port, but as I have said, in the end, we arrived in Palestine by air.

After I returned home, I thought my days of wandering abroad were over, and now the Haganah would let me contribute my part to fighting the war. Encouraged by Yigal Allon, I expressed my desire to fight in the Palmach. But after only a few days, I was summoned by Israel Galili, to be told I had been "sentenced" to another mission abroad. Galili invited me to lunch at the Tnuva Restaurant on Frishman Street near the Red House in Tel Aviv, where the offices of the minister of defense, the chief of the Haganah, and the branches of the General Staff were located. Over lunch, Galili told me about the purchase of aircraft from abroad: the Czechoslovakian government had sold us Messerschmitt fighter planes and had also offered us additional aircraft of various types, both civilian and military. However, because of the war, it was first necessary to bring the fighter planes to Palestine to protect the other planes that would be parked in the various airfields and to provide air cover and backup for the ground forces. Only once the fighter planes were in place could we bring the other types of aircraft.

I realized that the chief of the Haganah understood why I resisted the idea of leaving the country again at such a fateful time, but he explained the urgency of the mission: "You have to leave for Europe immediately to get things organized and to dispatch to us the planes we bought in recent months as quickly as possible. There's no choice because we haven't yet found a way to bring them here." Previous attempts by Yitzhak Levi, Freddy Pratkin, and Yehoshua Gilutz to fly them to Palestine had failed. In a chance meeting on the steps of the Red House, Levi and Gilutz told me about those failures and expressed their doubts that I'd be able to cope with the problems that would arise, because of limitations imposed by Shaul Avigur as well as the logistical obstacles that the airlift entailed. Their comments were not exactly encouraging.

At the end of our conversation, Galili promised that my stay in Europe would not be long. He gave me a letter for Avigur, who was coordinating arms procurement in Europe, which set forth the essence of my mission. I overcame my reluctance to leave again, since all my reasons for staying paled in comparison to the weighty points raised by Galili, who I knew would never stoop to simply pulling rank. Moreover, the defense minister was party to Galili's decision. I consulted Yigal Allon, too, as to whether I should accept this mission; Allon expressed the view that bringing the fighter planes to the country was far more important than any other role I could play in the war itself.

The fighting in Israel was at its peak. On the morning of May 15, Tel Aviv was bombed from the air, as were the airfields in which the few small planes we had (the *Primusim*, named for the Primus [kerosene] heaters of which they were reminiscent) stood parked. Since we lacked fighter planes that could intercept enemy aircraft, our airfields were easy bombing targets. This shortcoming caused all our vital centers and large population concentrations to be easy marks for enemy planes. The latter were in no great danger flying over Israel since at the time all we had were a few Oerlikon 20-caliber anti-aircraft guns (made by Hispano Suissa, a Swiss arms manufacturer). Indeed, the frequency and scope of the bombings got worse and worse, and our helplessness burned in the hearts of our fighters. Furthermore, our small planes weren't allowed to take off out of fear that they might encounter the enemy fighter planes. Even before the formal invasion by the Arab armies, the Haganah established airborne observation patrols to keep track of our enemies' movements and to rush reinforcements and supplies to settlements in distress; however, the supremacy of the Egyptian air force was felt in all of the campaigns of the war.

Finding a plane to fly me out of the country was no simple matter as the regular airlines had canceled all their flights to Israel. One day, a Beechcraft airplane landed in Israel. It had been leased by a group of French journalists who had come to cover the war. We immediately rented the plane for a flight to Europe. The Beechcraft was set to take off for Paris from the airport in Haifa, since at that time the road from Tel Aviv to the Lod airport was closed to us following attacks on the road by Arab gangs and villagers. The Beechcraft was scheduled to land at several other airports on its way to Paris in order to take on fuel, but since there was no way for me to get to Prague on a direct flight, there was no choice but to fly this indirect route. Scheduled to leave on the same plane were Golda Meir, sent by Ben-Gurion to the United States to raise funds for the war; Teddy Kollek, who headed the Haganah delegation in the United States; and Gideon Rafael, who was on a diplomatic mission to the United States.

On the day of the flight, I arrived at David Ben-Gurion's house at 4 A.M., at his request. His wife Paula, who opened the door for me, refused to let me in at such an early hour, but when Ben-Gurion heard us talking, he came down from the second floor in his underwear and ushered me in. He told me how crucial he and the IDF High Command considered this mission which involved organizing the airlift of the warplanes, recruiting flight crews in the States and in Europe, manning the planes, and transferring the weapons out of Czechoslovakia, other European nations, and the United States. He urged me to reach my destination as soon as possible and to inform Avigur of his decision to give this effort the highest priority of all of our activities in Europe. I was also to deliver several messages from him to Avigur and to Ehud Avriel—prognoses for the course of the war, and his opinions of a number of people, which I promised not to reveal to anyone but Avigur.

As we were sitting in the plane and the engines were starting, a messenger suddenly came running to tell me that a Czech DC-3 (Dakota) was due to land soon at the Haifa airport and was scheduled to return to Prague the same day. After conferring with Golda and Teddy, I decided to get off the French plane and wait for the Czech one.

The hours of waiting for the Czech plane seemed interminable. The fear that I might not get to my destination quickly enough gnawed at me. To my relief, my concerns were groundless and the plane arrived around noon. I reached Prague the same day, and as soon as I got there I held a preliminary consultation with the heads of the Haganah delegation in Czechoslovakia—Ehud Avriel, Yehuda Ben-Horin (Brigger) of Kibbutz Hazorea. The consultation took place in Hotel Esplanade where Ehud Avriel was staying.

Among Avriel's team of assistants in Czechoslovakia were Levi Argov (Kopelevich) and Hanan Guy. Avigur and Avriel had appointed Argov commander of the airport at Zatech. Guy, the Institution for Clandestine Immigration's specialist in sailing vessels and shipping, assisted Ehud in various missions. There was another man with them, named Ish-Shalom, a member of Hashomer Hatza'ir, born in Czechoslovakia, who had coordinated rescue missions there during World War II.

Yehuda Ben-Horin saw to flying transports of arms and organized Operation Balak—the arms shipments by air from Czechoslovakia to Israel during the war. In its early stages, the operation was based on an American 4-engine DC-4 (Skymaster), leased by the Haganah in Europe from its American owner. Ben-Horin became friendly with the members of the crew and won their confidence, and they had managed to fly out two loads of arms by the time I arrived in Czechoslovakia. He ortchestrated the airlifting of the Czech arms (machine guns, rifles, other types of weapons, and ammunition), an operation that played a decisive role in the months leading up to the establishment of the state and in the initial stages of the War of Independence. Avriel and Ben-Horin were the planners and organizers, that is, the moving force and the spirit behind the building of the infrastructure upon which the missions of Balak were based. Ben-Horin was personally involved in the entire gamut of activities that every sortie entailed, and principally the loading of the weapons, making contact with the crew and briefing them, liaising with the commander of the Ajaccio (Corsica) airport to ensure the refueling en route to Israel, and getting backup from him to conceal the flight's destinations. The Jewish Agency representative in France, a man named Fisher, made the contact with the French authorities and obtained their agreement to our using the airport at Corsica.

Ben-Gurion and Galili assigned me the mission of delivering the Messerschmitts and organizing their airlift, for which we used the C-46 and the Constellation aircraft that Haganah emissaries had procured in the United States and smuggled into Mexico and

Panama before the imposition of the strict embargo on shipments of arms and aircraft from the United States to Israel. Foremost among these emissaries was Al Schwimmer, the American pilot who became the central figure in all the activities of the Haganah and its delegation—in procuring the planes and recruiting the flight crews needed to conduct the airlift from Czechoslovakia and for the air force in Israel. But this historic, unprecedented operation could not have succeeded but for the teamwork and spirit of cooperation of the workers, during the organizational phases and throughout the entire period of the airlift. The latter included some fifteen cargo planes of various sizes and models, which flew fighter planes (including fifty Spitfires purchased from Czechoslovakia at a later stage), bombs, weapons, ammunition, and other equipment, and in which a few dozen flight crews, maintenance technicians, escorts, liaisons, and other functionaries took part.

All those who had the privilege of witnessing the landing of the first planes of Operation Balak couldn't help but feel that a great historic drama was unfolding before their eyes at the Beit Daras airport. Those first sorties were the turning point in the Yishuv's ability to stand firm in the face of the onslaught by forces that were but a few steps short of fulfilling their malicious designs.

The planes landed at an absolutely critical moment just as doubts were starting to creep into the hearts of the Yishuv leaders and combatants. They wondered whether they would have the strength to thwart these designs without the military material due to arrive on the planes, as well as the first shipments that had arrived on a Danish boat that came from Italy and the boats *Nora* and *Shayo* from Czechoslovakia.

Working with Avriel was Uriel "Felix" Doron who had immigrated to Palestine from Czechoslovakia. Felix had studied in Prague. While he was in school, he became close friends with some of those who were to fill senior positions in the future Czech government. Later he was appointed a representative in the Israeli embassy in Prague and it was mostly on Felix that Avriel relied to develop ties with that country's top leadership. Of special importance were the ties formed with the General Secretary of the Communist Party, the Foreign Ministry, Defense Ministry, and especially the Czech State Bank, since with the credit obtained from the bank the purchases of more Messerschmitts and other arms, and fifty Spitfires that were purchased later, were financed.

Avriel was one of the people closest to Ben-Gurion, and he was in the upper echelons of the clandestine immigration organization headed by Shaul Avigur. Yehuda Braginsky and Shaike Dan were considered the architects of the contacts with the countries of Eastern Europe, where they labored to procure weapons and to smuggle Jews into Palestine.

Avriel's ties with the countries of Eastern Europe were formed in the 1930s and continued through the period when he was operating in Istanbul, in the early years of World War II. He worked with the Jewish Agency representative Haim Barless and Teddy Kollek to make contacts with Jewish communities and Zionist organizations in German-occupied lands and to initiate operations to rescue as many Jews as possible. Avriel was the first to welcome Joel Brand, who had been sent by Eichmann's representatives in Hungary to advance the "blood for goods deal," and he tried to transport him from Istanbul to Palestine. Brand was arrested by the British at the Syrian border and was then transferred to Cairo for interrogation.

Earlier efforts made by people who came to Prague before Avriel showed that the ground in Czechoslovakia was ripe for extensive arms procurement. The Czechs' cooperativeness was ascribed to the positive and surprising about-face in the Soviet Union's position on Palestine, an about-face that was reflected in the deliberations at the United Nations, in which the Soviet Union, together with the United States, supported the Partition Plan and the establishment of a Jewish state—one of the rare instances, if not the only one, of

United States-Soviet accord during the Cold War. This reversal constituted the cornerstone of Soviet policy in the Middle East at that time and was expressed in the dramatic speech of Andrei Gromyko, Soviet Foreign Minister, at the General Assembly of the United Nations. Discussions that we had with officials in the Czech government and other Communist nations gave us the impression that the decision that lay behind this reversal in Soviet policy was made in Stalin's Politburo, although this impression never received official verification.

Airlifting the Messerschmitts

In my first meeting with Ehud Avriel and Yehuda Ben-Horin in Prague, I gave them Galili's letter* and explained the goals of my mission. We carefully examined our various options for airlifting the first nine Messerschmitts that had already been bought and paid for. We concluded that the fighter planes couldn't possibly make the entire flight to Israel without any stopovers. The Messerschmitt had a relatively short range, and the amount of time it could remain airborne was limited. It would need to make stopovers for refueling, but we did not yet have access to airports, with the exception of one French airport on the island of Corsica. We had a special relationship with this airport's commander, who gave us his cooperation.

---

* The full contents of the letter are as follows:
  "To Or [Avigur's nom de guerre], Shalom!
  "Without fighter planes and bombers it is possible that we won't be defeated, but we will never achieve victory in this war, nor will we save settlements and whole sections of territory from falling to the enemy.
  "The enemy has six Spitfires. In a meeting with Amitai [Ben-Gurion's *nom de guerre*], we decided that Eliyahu S. will go abroad with a single mission: to get the planes already purchased to Palestine. Inform all of our people that for this job—the speedy delivery of the planes we have bought—Eliyahu has absolute authority. He will act in accordance with your instructions. We expect you to give him every possible assistance.
  "Hillel [Galili's *nom de guerre*]"

Our pressing need to find an additional airport where we could land closer to Israel was apparent. After strenuous efforts by Ehud and Shaike Dan, the Yugoslavian authorities gave us landing rights at one of their country's airports. However, this permission was only obtained at a later stage; until that time, we sought another way to airlift the Messerschmitts with no stopovers.

The only workable solution we could find originally was to fly the components of disassembled Messerschmitts in transport planes with a capacity large enough to hold one or two planes. After much deliberation, we decided to designate our DC-4 for this purpose, even though this meant a temporary cessation of arms deliveries. But we didn't know if our people in Israel would be able to reassemble the planes fast enough to get them ready for battle. After all, at that time our air force did not yet have technicians or ground services, and certainly not specialists in the assembly of Messerschmitts.

The DC-4 arrives at the Zatech airport

We decided to explain our problems to our Czech negotiating partners, hoping they would agree to send their own team of specialists to Israel, to help with the reassembly. To our great surprise, within a few hours we got an affirmative answer, and the main obstacle to carrying out our plan had been removed. We contacted Israel right away, got the approval of the chief of the Haganah, the defense minister, and the commander of the air force (Aharon Remez), and set about arranging and preparing for the airlift of our first fighter plane.

About that same time, the DC-4 was undergoing minor renovations in Paris, and Yehuda Ben-Horin flew there to enable him to return the same day to "our" airfield—the Czech government had put a military airfield near the town of Zatech, about a four hour drive from Prague, at our disposal. The field was closed to all civilian traffic, Czech military guards were posted all around it, and only those with special permits were admitted. Without a doubt, this arrangement was the key factor in the success of our operation, and the base from which we were able to build our airlift.

During the same period, espionage rings of countries hostile to Israel were active in Europe, including in Czechoslovakia. The American embassy in Prague was also keeping an eye on us, showing special interest in the considerable number of teams of Americans, both Jews and non-Jews, at the center of our activities. One problem the Czech government and we faced was how to conceal the fact that American teams were present on Czech soil. This was no simple matter considering the customary behavior of pilots, and particularly American pilots, who tended to spend their leisure time in clubs and entertainment spots near airports.

As I have said, in our first transaction nine planes were sold to us, and they were flown from the factory in Brno to "our" airfield. At our request, in the first stage a formation of three planes was handed over to us. At the field, we held a ceremony "welcoming" the first Messerschmitts, which was attended by a party of experts, engineers, technical workers, and representatives of the Czech government and army. The technicians and experts set to work right away. They set up a temporary workshop at the field, equipped with all the tools and equipment needed to disassemble the planes.

Our preliminary calculations gave us reason to hope no major problems would arise with getting the disassembled airplane parts into the DC-4. Still, there was some anxiety about possible miscalculations or overlooking of crucial details, and that reality might backfire on us. Our main concern was that the fuselage was relatively clumsy to handle and that it was just about the size of the transport plane's opening. We were afraid the fuselage would get stuck going through the opening, making it impossible to insert it into the DC-4.

There was no problem loading the propeller or the wings—that phase went without a hitch. The DC-4 was a true transport plane whose opening was extremely wide. The technicians set up a special crane, which lifted each plane segment to the height of the aircraft's opening. Then we carefully pushed the part into the plane. We placed wooden boards on the floor of the DC-4 to protect the aircraft parts from being scratched or otherwise damaged. But the fuselage was something else again. After repeated attempts, we realized there was no way to get the body of the Messerschmitt into the transport using the same method. Someone suggested turning the fuselage around, tail first, but we had no better luck with that approach. Fortunately, the Czechs refused to give up and kept trying, until suddenly, as night was about to fall and we were verging on despair, the miracle happened: In some strange way, without any particular supervision, the fuselage slid gracefully into the DC-4.

We gave a roar of happiness—we were actually starting to believe the Messerschmitts would arrive in Israel in time. We loaded all the appropriate types of weapons and a large quantity of ammunition onto the plane as well and added a significant number of bombs as the Messerschmitt also served as a fighter bomber.

After we finished the loading, the DC-4 took off on its direct flight from Zatech to Akir (Ekron), the Haganah's airfield. We sent word home by wireless, informing them that the plane had taken off with the State of Israel's first fighter plane, and that aboard were also two pilots who had completed their Messerschmitt training course in Czechoslovakia. One of these pilots was Ezer Weismann, a future air force commander and President of the State of Israel, and the second was Modi Allon, who was killed when his plane was hit in combat.

Before Nightfall—Another Takeoff

We prepared to fly the Czech technical team out as soon as the plane left, to keep from losing precious time in assembling the planes. Before anything else, we briefed the technicians, explained the problems to them, and promised them every possible assistance in their work in Israel. They were flown to Israel in the plane that transported the third Messerschmitt because the experts thought it important to have at least three planes already in Israel, which could constitute an effective combat unit.

The round-trip flight from Zatech to Israel took about twenty-four hours. It was risky to fly continuously without allowing the DC-4 crew time to rest but there was no alternate crew. However, from what the Czechs said, and from the course the war was taking in Israel, we concluded that we had to make a supreme effort and to complete the airlift of the first three planes in as rapid a series of flights as possible.

Still, it was clear that we wouldn't be able to manage with only one plane for the airlift operation. We knew that the crew couldn't long endure the superhuman effort of continuous flying without rest; so I decided to recruit additional planes, to speed up the pace of the airlifts and to quickly complete delivery of all the nine Messerschmitts that we had purchased.

Some C-46 airplanes came to our rescue. Yehuda Arazi, Teddy Kollek, and Al Schwimmer had purchased them in the United States, and our people managed to get them into Mexico and Panama before the American embargo went into effect. The same night we decided that one transport plane was not enough, I phoned Teddy Kollek in the States and asked him for Al Schwimmer's help to send us all of these planes so that we might set up an airlift from Czechoslovakia to Israel.

Since we had received instructions from Israel to fly the C-46 directly to Israel, I felt an obligation to contact Avigur in Geneva as well as the High Command to get their approval for my plan. I explained that it would be better to concentrate a larger number of fighter planes in Israel, to protect the airfields from air attacks, and only then to fly the C-46s, plus two Constellations, which had also been smuggled into Mexico and Panama, to Israel.

A further rationale that I gave them was that besides transporting

Messerschmitts, the c-46s and the Constellations could serve as an infrastructure for the airlift and as a logistics system by means of which we could quickly send arms to Israel and supply the IDF's other urgent needs. After only a few hours, we got the authorization for our plans.

At dawn the next day, we received word that the DC-4 had landed safely at Akir, thus crowning with success the first phase in our mission of airlifting the fighter planes. After a few hours we received a congratulatory telegram from the minister of defense and the chief of the Haganah saying that this operation had opened a new chapter in the operations of the Haganah and the IDF abroad. All of this happened on May 19, 1948.

Encouraged by our success, we began intensive preparations to airlift the rest of the Messerschmitts. The DC-4 had returned from Israel to "our" airfield in Czechoslovakia, and though the crew was exhausted, we explained to them how important it was not to waste any time. The crew agreed to our request that they take off for a second flight without delay, grabbing only a brief rest while the second Messerschmitt was being loaded onto the DC-4. This time, now that our workers were experienced, the loading of the plane parts went smoothly. The Czech technicians and workers became quite expert, and from one sortie to the next, the loading time got shorter and shorter.

Before nightfall, the DC-4 took off on its second expedition. There were some more men who had completed the course in piloting Messerschmitts, and in accordance with the instructions of the commander of the air force and the minister of defense, who wanted them in Israel without delay, they flew back with the second Messerschmitt, serving as a living communications link with Israel. They carried with them my letters and reports on the course of the operation and the problems we had to solve.

When I got back to my hotel, a telegram from Teddy Kollek was waiting for me stating that our first c-46 had already left Panama.

We were overjoyed, knowing how helpful this would be for speeding up the airlift.

The Volunteers from America

The way in which our representatives overcame the difficulties, legal and otherwise, that flying the "Panamanian" and "Mexican" planes from one country to another entailed is a story unto itself. Suffice it to say that the planes managed to take off and to arrive in Europe in coordination with the commander of the airfield in Corsica, having made some stops on the way to refuel.

"Our" crew arrived with the first plane—Jewish and non-Jewish pilots from the United States, who had volunteered to serve in the Haganah and became the backbone of the airlift. Most of them were well-known pilots with many years of experience in the American air force.

The progress and expansion of our activities, the momentum that our air force gained in Israel, and its appearance as a fighting force at such an early stage in the war, could not have happened, were it not for the decisive role played by these volunteers, and their limitless dedication. Subsequently, they shouldered the technical and administrative burdens and maintenance of the aircraft.

The pilot who stood out from all the rest was Sam Pomerantz, whom we called "The Walking Encyclopedia," in deference to his amazing knowledge about all aspects of aviation and aircraft maintenance. Aharon Remez, commander of the air force, took my advice about asking Pomerantz to assist in Israel in improving coordination between the Israeli air force and our operations at the Zatech airfield. He joined one of the flights and remained in Israel for four days, holding consultations and discussions with Aharon Remez and other senior commanders in the air force, after which, at my request, he returned to Zatech to continue working with the airlift.

The DC-4 crew members were paid professionals, and despite

their devoted service, we knew we couldn't base our activities in Israel and in Czechoslovakia on these men over the long term. So we asked the Haganah delegation in the United States to intensify its recruitment of pilots as much as possible in order to ensure that we would have "our own" crews on all the planes. But despite their best efforts, recruitment of volunteers proceeded slowly. A few more pilots came from the United States and we recruited three combat pilots in England, one of whom signed on in time to take part in the course in Czechoslovakia. This man was a deputy squadron leader in the RAF until a few days before the course started, and he managed to get leave. The two other English pilots were on their way from Italy to Czechoslovakia at the time. Two American pilots were then in training in the course in Czechoslovakia, and five others had completed their training and were about to leave for Israel. We had a grand total of thirteen fighter pilots (including three Israelis), some of whom were already in Israel. This number fell far short of meeting our needs, and we had to start a new recruitment effort in America and Europe.

Gradually, the flights became a matter of routine, which is not to say that problems didn't occur every now and then. Undeniably, a key factor in our success was the Czech government's sympathetic attitude toward us and the fact that they put everything we needed to realize this complex and multi-faceted operation at our disposal.

The C-46s, whose fuel capacity was too small for a long flight— such as a direct flight from Czechoslovakia to Israel—had to take on more fuel en route. This service could be performed at the airfield in Corsica, with whose commander, as I have said, we enjoyed close cooperation.

Now that we had five more C-46s that we could put onto a regular flight schedule, we could give the crews time to rest between flights. At this same time, there were two Constellation aircraft in

Panama, also purchased by Al Schwimmer and Yehuda Arazi in the United States and flown to Panama before the American embargo went into effect. These planes were flown from Panama to Zatech. The first was damaged while landing, but the crew were unhurt. The second joined the airlift. At the same time, the ground services were getting organized, though we still suffered from a lack of manpower.

Every Messerschmitt was loaded with a quantity of weapons and bombs, but it was necessary to fly additional large amounts of these in order to keep the fighter planes equipped without interruption. Thus, shipments of the various types of arms started up again in accordance with the orders sent to the delegation. In this way, our flight path became an airlift in the full sense of the word. Thanks to the airlift, our army quickly began to obtain the arms and ammunition it needed, for the Messerschmitts as well as for other urgent defense needs.

I believe our airlift can be described as a miniature of the Berlin airlift in 1948, although ours preceded that larger airlift, although the American and British airlift was operated out in the open, while our operations were clandestine.

The airlifting of the Messerschmitts was not without mishap. One of the first nine Messerschmitts was lost when the c-46 carrying it crashed. The tragedy occurred at the Akir airfield: The plane arrived towards dawn while a thick fog blanketed the field. Apparently, the pilot was not guided properly by the flight controllers and crashed upon landing. The c-46 went up in flames together with the Messerschmitt parts it was carrying. The crew managed to escape, with the exception of the captain, Moses Aaron Rosenbaum, who was killed. Rosenbaum was one of the pillars of our activity, and his loss saddened us greatly. He was born in the United States, but he turned out to really be "one of us," and served as a model of dedication, modesty, and courage.

The heroism of the anonymous men who brought the tools of battle to our fighters in the days when the newborn Israel was struggling with its back to the sea, deserves the nation's esteem and gratitude. These few men gave us the indispensable means to set out on campaigns of victory. There is no question that historians and analysts who study the history of the War of Independence in depth will also stress the role played by the airlift from Czechoslovakia and its share in the sum total of factors that contributed to the IDF's victory. A copy of my letter to the commander of the air force, Major General Eitan Ben-Eliyahu, on this subject may be found in Appendix A.

To return to the airlift of the Messerschmitts: At the same time that the first squadron was being flown to Israel, Ehud Avriel reached an agreement with the Czech authorities concerning the purchase of additional Messerschmitts, Spitfires, and weapons, paid for partly in cash, with the remainder financed on credit granted by the Czech State Bank.

The airlift that we established and operated together with the heroism and the spirit of sacrifice of the fighters, gave the IDF breathing space in the war against overwhelming forces, and equipped it with a significant share of the tools and the arms that made possible the shift from defensive battles to large-scale offensives, and even tilted the balance of the war.

Some time later, when I returned from the United States to Czechoslovakia after smuggling the "Flying Fortresses" (B-17s) into Israel, I stayed in Prague at the Alkron Hotel. A number of Arabs from other Middle Eastern countries, including Egypt and Syria, were also staying there, apparently working at the embassies of their countries in Prague. The theatrical director Joseph Milo, who became friendly with some of the Arabs, was staying at the same hotel. When I arrived at the hotel, he told me that he heard from them about the first bombing mission of the Flying Fortresses and about the shockwaves that event sent through their countries.

During that stay in Prague, I learned that Israel Galili had come to the resort town of Marienbad after David Ben-Gurion decided to eliminate the job of chief of the Haganah. This meant the dismissal of Galili, who took the decision very hard. As soon as I could, I went to visit him and his wife, Tzipporah. He told me all the details about what led to this move, and it was impossible not to feel Galili's depression after being hurt so badly. Nevertheless, I sensed that he was cheered somewhat by my report about the successful launch of the Flying Fortresses, Al Schwimmer's and Teddy Kollek's extensive activities to recruit air crews and technicians for ground services and the airlift that was now making regular runs from Czechoslovakia.

The Flying Course in Czechoslovakia

Before my arrival in Czechoslovakia to organize the airlift of the Messerschmitts to Israel, Ehud Avriel had obtained the Czech Defense Ministry's agreement to set up a flying school for Israelis and foreign volunteers to train them in the operation of the Messerschmitts that we had purchased. I had the opportunity to visit the school, accompanied by Avriel and by Uriel "Felix" Doron and to get an idea of the progress of the training and of the personalities of the students. Our impression was that the studies were not going smoothly and that progress was slower than we were hoping for.

The course of studies and training prepared by the staff was based on the assumption that all the participants had received combat experience in World War II. Accordingly, the thrust of the program was a concerted and accelerated effort whose essence was to give the students the necessary experience and training in the operation of the Messerschmitt and skipped over the primary stages of flight studies.

Ehud Avriel told me that he called this fact to the attention of our people in Israel and that they assured him that the students would be chosen and screened accordingly. However, once the course started, the instructors realized there was a vast difference between the American pilots, with their significant combat experience from World War II, and the Israeli participants. As a result, the staff of the school was forced to divide the students into three groups: Americans with combat experience, who completed their training within a few days; four advanced Israelis, who started their training at an advanced stage; and three Israeli beginners, who had to start with the basics.

After two weeks of regular training the colonel in charge of the course summoned our proxy, and while he praised the spirit, motivation, and willpower of the Israeli men, he expressed doubt that they were up to the task of flying fighter planes, both due to their limited experience and to their relatively advanced age. He recommended enlisting more pilots from America or other nations with combat experience. To support his view, the colonel pointed to the first five American pilots, who had already completed their training and gained complete technical and operational mastery of the Messerschmitt, while the other trainees were far behind. In our discussion, the colonel emphasized the special difficulties of this plane and of mastering it and said our people would be ready to fly it only after a long training period.

Avriel was resistant to putting a stop to the training of our men, and he persuaded the colonel to continue with them for the time being. For their part, our men, who were impatient and hoped to learn came to the realization that willpower and determination were not enough and that they would have to get used to the idea of lengthy and systematic training.

The instructors were hesitant to let them fly solo and resisted the pressures our people tried to apply. But finally they broke down and agreed to one solo flight. Pinyeleh Ben-Porat, a member of Kibbutz Na'an, was the one chosen for this attempt. Everyone considered Ben-Porat the outstanding student in this group. His attempt ended in a crash landing, although Ben-Porat came out of the accident with only light injuries. This mishap increased the reservations of the colonel, and he summoned us for a consultation on the future training of this class. After again praising the personal qualities and intelligence of our men, he repeated that these traits were not enough to equip them to operate the Messerschmitt in regular flight, not to mention in combat.

Following this discussion, we conferred with our men. The fact that they kept their spirits up even after Pinyeleh's accident impressed us. Nevertheless, probably thanks to the accident, they acknowledged that the colonel was right and that they would have to realize that their learning to be combat pilots was going to take longer than they had expected at the outset. It was our impression that the colonel was not in favor of calling off the course either. After ascertaining the students' state of mind, we had another discussion with the colonel and convinced him to continue the course.

The colonel met with his students and suggested that they devote two weeks to training in a two-seater airplane, followed by another week of training with the Messerschmitt. The men were happy with this "phased plan" and agreed to it immediately.

I made my position clear to them: They had to continue their training, hard as it might be, since the State of Israel needed an air force with a nucleus of Israelis. Not that we weren't grateful for each and every American pilot, but we couldn't consider them the backbone of our air force and the shapers of its image. Avriel spoke along similar lines, although the truth is, the boys had plenty of motivation even without our pep talk.

After our discussion, we went to visit Ben-Porat in the hospital, where we were happy to see that the accident had left his self-confidence and his decision to continue with his training unshaken. At the end of the war, Ben-Porat went on to work as a captain with El Al.*

At the same time, a beginners flying course was also being conducted in Italy. I was devoting all my time and efforts then to airlifting the Messerschmitts and other cargoes, and I couldn't visit there, but our people told me that the course was not proceeding satisfactorily, and that it would be more useful and effective to transfer the course for beginners to Czechoslovakia. I so advised the chief of General Staff and the Commander of the Air Force, Aharon Remez, and indeed a few students were transferred from the course in Italy to our flight school in Czechoslovakia.

Ehud Avriel, head of the arms purchasing mission in Czechoslovakia in 1948

* He was killed with all of his passengers in 1955 when his plane was hit by Bulgarian fighter planes while on its way to Israel. This cruel act should probably be seen in the context of the Cold War. It developed into an international diplomatic incident and affected Israel's relationship with Bulgaria.

The author's wife and their two daughters in Prague at the time the "aerial railroad" was organized in 1948

The Purchase of the Flying Fortresses (B-17s) and Flying in Secret from the United States

While we were putting the first squadron of nine planes into operation, I couldn't stop thinking how crucial it was for us to procure bombers. This was not only because of their strategic and military importance, but also for the psychological effect that would come with having them in the air. I thought that the appearance of heavy bombers above our battlefields was likely to deal a heavy psychological and moral blow to the enemy, and it seemed to me that doing so was no less important than the operational advantage of these planes. Nachum "Sergei" Sarig of the Palmach Negev Brigade wrote me a letter which attests to the effect the arrival of the Messerschmitts had on the course of the war. Sergei was there for the planes' maiden sortie, when they came to the aid of the ground forces and provided them cover. The letter appears in Appendix B.

Our efforts to purchase Halifax, Mosquito, Lancaster, and similar bombers in Europe failed. One possibility remained open to us: to buy American bombers that had been stripped of their weapons and sold to merchants at the end of World War II. Thus, as soon as the airlift of the first squadron of Messerschmitts was completed and the organization, apparatus, and administrative-technical infrastructure were in place at the Zatech airfield, I decided to direct all my attention to acquiring bombers.

Such an idea seemed wild and unrealistic under the circumstances of the times. It was no wonder that some of the people with whom I discussed it were skeptical to the point that they considered it quixotic. I turned to Ehud Avriel to discuss turning over my job to Yehuda Ben-Horin so that I could concentrate on getting our hands on some bombers. He thought the idea was good, but then I had to convince Shaul Avigur, who at that time was responsible for all Haganah and arms purchasing activities in Europe.

Yehuda Ben-Horin took over the responsibility for the continuation of the airlift operation of the Messerschmitts as well as Czech and other arms while I set out to visit Avigur in Hotel Angléter in Geneva. I updated Avigur on the progress of the airlift, told him about the extensive organization we had set up in Czechoslovakia, and presented my plan to him: to go to the United states, try to purchase bombers, and fly them to Israel as quickly as possible. At first he wasn't crazy about the idea. Previous attempts at purchasing weapons in the United States had ended in failure and considerable sums of money had gone down the drain. Above all, he didn't believe it would be possible to bypass the strict American embargo on arms shipments, military equipment, and strategic raw materials from the United States to Israel.

The arguments, explanations, and discussions continued for most of the night. It was nearly morning when Avigur was finally convinced that the plan was worth trying. Perhaps the decisive point was that we had no alternative source for purchasing bombers—even if our efforts were in vain, we had nothing to lose by trying. I convinced Avigur that Ben-Horin could fill in for me and continue overseeing the airlifting of arms to Israel. I had the backing of the minister of defense and the chief of General Staff, as well as the encouragement of Teddy Kollek, head of the Haganah delegation in the United States, who by phone promised me all the help I'd need to carry out the mission. I told Avigur that I had written to the minister of defense, the chief of General Staff, and the Air Force commander Aharon Remez, suggesting that if we succeeded in getting bombers and arming them at the airfield in Czechoslovakia, they could bomb strategic targets in Egypt on their way to Israel. Extensive details on this idea were included in reports that I sent from Czechoslovakia to the minister of defense, the chief of the Haganah, and to Aharon Remez.

The Zatech airfield was a key factor in the plan, since it would be inconceivable to fly a bomber, even a four-engine piston, all the way from the United States to Israel without a stopover. Moreover, the B-17 bombers were stripped of their weapons, and there was no way to arm and equip them with arms and bombs in Israel. This could only be done at the airfield in Czechoslovakia.

So in early June 1948, I left for the United States to buy Flying Fortresses (B-17s), arrange for their being flown to the Zatech airfield, where they would be armed and equipped with bombs and then flown to Israel. In America I recruited Yosef Eitan (Joe Eisen), who had previously worked as Yehuda Arazi's assistant and was about to return to Israel. He told me where I could find Al Schwimmer, whom I hoped to enlist to help with the operation.

Al Schwimmer, together with Hank Greenspan, was then in Mexico conducting negotiations with the Mexican government to purchase Mexican arms. I asked him to come to Houston, Texas, where I told him about the airlift of the Messerschmitts and the arms from Czechoslovakia to Israel, by means of the DC-4 and a few C-46s, which Schwimmer and Kollek had sent in answer to my request. I told him, too, that all our attempts to acquire bombers in Europe had failed, and that our last remaining source was the United States. I added that the minister of defense, the chief of General Staff, and Golda Meir supported the operation, and that

Meir had been sent by Ben-Gurion to raise funds in America to finance the war.

Schwimmer (the central figure in all activity connected with the acquisition of aircraft and getting them out of the United States, the purchase of spare parts, and recruitment of flight crews) worked with Teddy Kollek in the United States to recruit pilots, navigators, and engineers, both Jews and non-Jews. I emphasized how important it was for him to join us in our efforts to acquire bombers, in view of his vast experience, his past service in the American air force, and his many contacts with flight and navigation crews. Schwimmer did indeed respond positively to our request and became the central figure of the operation. He negotiated for the purchase of the bombers, recruited the flight crews, and played a decisive role in creating the conditions necessary for the flight itself. At this stage we were helped by another American Jew, who instructed and trained us in the procedures required for getting planes air-borne from the airport.

Schwimmer, assisted by his hand-picked team, made contact with a few metal and junk dealers who had purchased large quantities of Flying Fortresses from the United States army, stripped of their weapons and ammunition. He eventually closed a deal with one of these dealers for an option to buy our first ten planes. If all went well, more planes would be purchased, Schwimmer implied. The cover story was that Schwimmer and his people were about to set up an air freight company, using these planes.

For reasons of caution, and as a first test of our plans we decided initially to fly three planes. Following the various checks and overhaul, the planes were flown to the Miami airport. All of a sudden, I received an order to hold up the flight, since the foreign ministry in Israel was afraid of the political repercussions if the operation should fail or its cover be breached. The people at the ministry were concerned about our delicate relationship with the

American Foreign Office and the risk of endangering that relationship. Ben-Gurion gave Golda Meir the authority to decide whether to go through with the airlift.

The debate took place at the Salgrave Hotel in New York where Meir was staying. The meeting was attended by Meir, Abba Eban, Teddy Kollek, and me. After a lengthy debate, Meir decided that we had to go through with the mission. If my memory serves currectly, she said: "On the scales are the fate, future, the very life of our people—accordingly, we cannot shrink from any risk involved in this chance to give to the IDF a strategic arm in its war against the Arab armies, an advantage likely to have a military and moral effect of great importance."

I went to the communication center of the Jewish Agency in New York to notify the chief of General Staff and the chief of the Haganah of the decision and then returned to Miami where we continued preparations for the flight. The price of the three Flying Fortresses waiting for us at the Miami airport was $30,000. Kollek sent me the money in a suitcase to the Fontainebleau Hotel in Miami via special messenger.

On the assigned day, the first two Fortresses took off at 4 A.M. from the Miami airport without any problems, but the third bomber had a blow-out in one of its tires as it was accelerating for take-off. The two planes already in the air had to circle above the city and wait for the third plane. The engine noise of the first two planes woke the citizens of Miami, and we were very anxious about the fate of the operation. We radioed the two bombers to fly some distance from the city and wait for the third plane, which took off as soon as the tire was changed, and joined the other two members of its formation.

The planes' first destination was the Azores Islands. After the planes refueled there, the captains declared that their next stop would be Corsica, but in reality they flew to our airfield in Czechoslovakia. According to our original plan, the commander of the airport in Corsica was to notify the airport in the Azores that the planes had landed safely at the appointed hour. However, for some reason, he did not receive the message I had sent him from New York, so that he failed to contact the airport in the Azores. When they received no word that the planes had landed in Corsica, they alerted the American air force and Coast Guard, who then began extensive searches. Of course, they did not turn up any sign of the Fortresses. The Americans became suspicious, and it didn't take long for them to conclude that the Haganah was involved in the affair. Front-page headlines blared that the Haganah was smuggling bombers out of the United States.

The Flying Fortresses landed at the Zatech airfield, were repaired and armed, and continued their flight. They received instructions to bomb Cairo en route to Israel. They did so, stupefying and shocking the Arab nations. Among the targets that they bombed in Cairo was the palace of King Farouk. This bombing operation was carried out in accordance with the plan that the chief of General Staff had approved while I was still in Czechoslovakia.

I would describe the crucial help we got from the Czechs as having occurred in two phases:

Stage 1: Light arms—the rifles, machine guns, and ammunition that started to flow from Czechoslovakia as described above, on the eve of the War of Independence and in its early stages, together with the weapons supplied by Ta'as and the underground arms shipments from Italy, Czechoslovakia, and other sources, lent the combat units the tools and the capability to halt the Arab armies and gave them breathing space to get past the initial phases of the war.

Stage 2: The Czechs supplied us with fighter planes and put at our disposal the air base at Zatech, which constituted the infrastructure for our logistics and made it possible to quickly supply arms, ammunition, bombs, fighter planes, bombers, and parts, without which our ability to withstand the onslaught of our enemies would have been inconceivable. All of the aforementioned, in addition to the weapons and ammunition supplied by Ta'as, formed the basis which enabled the IDF to go from defensive battles to major offensives, and ultimately to win the war.

Mr. Teddy Kollek, head of the "Haganah" and IDF mission in the years 1947–1949 and mayor of Jerusalem 1960–1995

David Hacohen and the Recruitment of Meir Sherman to the Haganah Delegation

In March 1948, when I was staying at the Commodore Hotel in New York, it was my practice to stop by every morning at the office of our delegation from Palestine at the Hotel Fourteen to discuss the progress of our work with Teddy Kollek. One morning I was surprised to see Leah Braun, one of Kollek's two secretaries, waiting at the entrance to the hotel. She motioned me aside and said she had word of a suspicious man who was in the office asking about me. His demeanor and his dress led them to suspect that he was an FBI agent. She described him as Hebrew-speaking, powerfully built and tall, wearing a hat and raincoat, and holding an umbrella. When he was told that I wasn't in the office, he produced a picture, asking that it be given to me so that I could identify him. He also wanted them to mention to me that his favorite poem was Bialik's "Hachnisini Tachat K'nafech Vahaii Li Em Ve'achot" ("take me under your wing and be a mother and a sister to me.")

As soon as she gave me the picture, I burst out laughing and told her the man was Meir Sherman, the son of Dr. Sherman, graduate of the Herzliya Gymnasium, who had been a member of the signal unit I had commanded when we were students. I went straight up to the office. Meir and I embraced and he told me that after he had completed his studies in the United States, he had obtained a job with a company named Anglo African, owned by a South African Jew named Jacobson, that dealt in international commerce. Sherman had risen steadily in the ranks and had been appointed to manage the American branch a few years earlier. I immediately realized we could use the man and his talents to great advantage for our work in the United States. This is the story:

One of the enterprises Teddy Kollek established in the United States was a company named Materials for Israel, which collected materials, objects, equipment, and even some American troop carriers, donated in large quantities by Jewish individuals and organizations in the United States. This company was headed by Victor Avrunin, an engineer who worked for Solel Boneh in Palestine, and once when he happened to be in the United States, Kollek gave him this job. Victor Avrunin had made *aliya* from America, and had ties with Golda Meir and with David Hacohen, the general manager of Solel Boneh. Meir Sherman expressed his desire to take on any job that might be assigned to him in the United States in the service of the provisional government even if he had to resign from his current job. It occurred to me that the extensive knowledge he had gained in the course of his work in the United States in commercial deals, shipments, negotiations, mastery of financial systems, and his Israeli background, could be important assets to the delegation's activities, and in particular they qualified him to head Materials for Israel. I introduced him to Kollek, they conversed, and my impression was that Kollek was interested in recruiting him. We came to the conclusion that Meir was gifted with qualities and talents that made him an excellent candidate to develop that enterprise and to give it a shot of adrenalin. While Victor Avrunin had proved his organizational and administrative ability beyond a doubt, it was plain to us that Meir Sherman had crucial experience, knowledge, and business contacts, and that this job was a perfect fit for him.

The main obstacle we had to overcome was that Avrunin enjoyed the vigorous support of David Hacohen as well as Meir's backing. We set about convincing Hacohen, who was in New York at the time, that Sherman's advantage over Avrunin was so great that it offset, at a time so fateful for the Jewish state, the inconvenience and unpleasantness involved in replacing the latter with the former.

We had some extremely agitated discussions with David Hacohen. I remember one in particular that took place as the two of us were walking down Fifth Avenue. We had just heard from our intelligence sources of the possibility of the Jordanian Legion joining the other Arab armies, which we knew would invade the country after the declaration of the establishment of the state. Hacohen expressed great anxiety at this possibility, concerned over the security situation in Palestine. I took advantage of his mood and once again brought up the idea of appointing Meir Sherman to head Materials for Israel. This time his response was more positive.

He invited me for a further conversation at his hotel. The following morning, when I arrived at his hotel, the door was opened by an attractive young woman. I was afraid that perhaps I had come on the wrong day or at the wrong time. After I regained my composure and told her my name, she showed me into the guest room and informed Hacohen. When he came in and saw my embarrassment, he evidently decided to leave me stewing and made no attempt to explain who the woman was and what she was doing in his suite at such an early hour.

Hacohen was always an amusing and fun-loving person who never missed an opportunity for a prank, practical joke, or other devilry, and seemed to get special pleasure out of embarrassing his friends. I realized from the mischievous gleam in his eye that I'd better be on alert. At the end of our conversation, as I was preparing to leave, he called the woman and introduced her to me as Aya Ruppin, sister of Carmela Ruppin, Yigal Yadin's wife. When I heard her name, I realized immediately why she had been in his flat: she was his niece.

How well I remember Hacohen teasing Eliyahu Golomb's children, David "Dodik", Dikla, and Dalia, when they were sitting in the living room, bent over their books and notebooks preparing their lessons amidst all the tumult in the house. Hacohen goaded them that their diligence was a waste of time; as proof he offered himself, saying he had never been particularly diligent in school, but that hadn't kept him from becoming the great David Hacohen, a cut far above the common folk. His humor and jokes delighted the children as they delighted everyone. Hacohen's personality was so likable, with not a trace of meanness or ill-will, that everyone who knew him took his jokes with good humor. What was special about him was his gift for breaking tension with funny stories and anecdotes. At the most difficult moments during the imprisonment of the Yishuv's leaders, this quality was a tremendous asset in that it lightened the tense atmosphere.

Hacohen was one of the pillars of security and economic activities in that period. He excelled in the power of his spirit and in his daring as a pioneer of the Zionist enterprise and as one of the drafters of policy toward the British authorities. After the establishment of the state, he served for quite a while as chair of the Knesset Foreign Affairs and Defense Committee and was appointed Israel's first ambassador to Burma.

Eventually, Kollek managed to orchestrate the personnel change, to enlist Meir Sherman, and to place him at the head of the vital organization. It is worth pointing out that Meir Sherman's willingness to accept this job and thus forgo a promising career, with boundless horizons, in the concern that he had managed in the United States, represented self-sacrifice on his part, from the standpoint both of his salary and standard of living, and of cutting off the business and managerial career that had been his for the taking in the world of commerce and finance. Meir Sherman became Kollek's right-hand man, and after he returned to Israel with his American wife and son, he held key economic posts in the state's institutions as one of Levi Eshkol's and Pinchas Sapir's most trusted aides and advisors.

Business people and economists with international experience were few and far between in government service after the founding of the state, and Meir Sherman became one of the central figures in the Ministry of Finance. He was even assigned, together with the American economist Oscar Gass, to conduct negotiations for our first loan from the United States, in the amount of $100 million, promised by the United States government to the government of Israel.

We can see in Meir Sherman one of the examples of voluntary activity arising from a profound sense of mission, to the extent of sacrificing one's own career and future. He was among those for whom material success was not always uppermost in their minds. When the British oil company Shell was purchased by Israel, Meir Sherman was appointed general manager of the government-owned company. After the company was privatized and became the Paz Company, Sherman returned to the United States, where he died of cancer at a relatively young age.

Arms Shipment From Mexico

While I was still in Czechoslovakia I heard from Ehud Avriel and other operatives about negotiations going on with a Mexican delegation with the objective of making a large purchase of various types of weapons.

When I arrived in the United States to arrange for the Flying Fortresses to be flown to Israel, Teddy Kollek told me in great detail about the talks being conducted by Hank Greenspan of Las Vegas and Al Schwimmer. Kollek noted that although matters had reached an advanced stage, they had come to an impasse because Shaul Avigur and Treasurer of Purchasing, Pino Ginsburg, who were in Geneva, had not yet approved the transaction and refused to authorize closing the deal and commitment to payment, as specified in the agreement with the Mexican delegation.

I heard further details on the developments in the negotiations from Al Schwimmer himself when we met in Houston, Texas, where I summoned him in order to get the delivery of the Flying Fortresses underway.

After the smuggling of the planes was discovered and reported in the American press, and the FBI started an investigation to discover who was involved in the mission, it became clear that I would have to leave the United States. But I lingered a few days in New York after sending, from the wireless communication center at the Jewish Agency offices, a report in code on the completion of the mission. I had to weigh whether to depart from the United States and return immediately to Israel or wait for instructions from Levi Eshkol, the director general of the Ministry of Defense. They had informed me that Pinhas Sapir (Avigur's replacement as coordinator of purchasing in Europe), backed by Ben-Gurion, wanted me to study the details of the arms deal in Mexico, to evaluate its progress and the position and intentions of those negotiating on behalf of the Mexican government, and to report to them what my conclusions were. Teddy Kollek was in favor and urged me to accept the assignment. He understood that Sapir and Ginsburg were skeptical about the negotiators' report that the deal was practical and feasible, so they held up the transfer of the money required to pay for the weapons.

Simultaneously, an arms dealer by the name of Larry Ives, who had been a colonel in the United States Marines in World War II, was trying to purchase fifty American tanks for us. Preliminary investigations by Kollek and others working for him indicated that there was a basis for such a deal. In the meantime, the tank deal reached an advanced stage: Colonel Ives managed to get an export license from the United States State Department, supposedly for the Mexican army. The export license cited Mexico as the end user, and according to the agreement with the Mexican government, the tanks were to be included in a comprehensive deal. The overall plan was to buy a ship in Canada and to bring it according to an agreed schedule to Tampico Bay, Mexico. There it was to be loaded with the Mexican weapons and the American tanks and weapons (machine guns, submachine guns, rifles, pistols, and ammunition) that Al Schwimmer and Hank Greenspan had assembled from various sources on the West Coast of the United States and that had been sent to Mexico.

Greenspan lived in Las Vegas and was owner and editor of the *Las Vegas Sun*. He was a close friend of the Jewish gangster, Bugsy Siegel, and even got Siegel to donate some of his own money and to raise additional funds for the Haganah from his many friends. Greenspan was a colorful character with ties to the elite of Las Vegas society. He readily agreed when Kollek and Schwimmer asked him to place himself at the Haganah's disposal. In the course of his activity on our behalf, he showed himself to be a man of courage and daring, resourceful, and an original thinker. He was tried in the United States after our War of Independence, on charges of illegal activity. He died a few years ago, and in his memory Teddy Kollek, Al Schwimmer, and the Greenspan family established a Jerusalem park in his name.

In one of Greenspan's and Schwimmer's more daring missions, they acquired arms on the West Coast of the United States and loaded them onto a yacht loaned to them by its Jewish owner in San Francisco Bay. One story that stands out in my mind took place when the yacht was on its way to Acapulco on the western coast of Mexico. The ship suddenly ran out of fuel and was stranded in the middle of the ocean. Greenspan swam to the Mexican shore and returned to the ship with a quantity of fuel that he managed to get in one of the villages. The cargo was so heavy that the yacht sank to the level of its rim. To our great good fortune, the Pacific lived up to its name and was very calm that day. It's not hard to imagine what might have happened if there had been a storm.

To return to our story: The first problem we had to solve was getting me a visa to enter Mexico, which not only had no diplomatic relations with Israel but was even hostile in the diplomatic arena due to the influence of its large Arab population. We were racing against the clock, and we knew we had to try our hardest to get a Mexican visa as quickly as possible.

While we were deliberating, Kollek thought of a wealthy Jewish businessman, one of the leaders of the Los Angeles Jewish community, who had shown outstanding dedication and loyalty to the Zionist cause. He had once told Kollek that he was a close friend of the Mexican consul in San Francisco. Kollek phoned this man immediately and explained the circumstances that made it necessary for me to get a visa to enter Mexico. It was agreed that I should travel to Los Angeles, where we would work together to obtain a visa.

He met me at the airport and took me to the Beverly Wilshire Hotel in an upscale area outside the city. When I stepped into the lobby, what greeted me was luxury and glamour the likes of which I had never seen in my life. This hotel was a favorite of Hollywood stars, the aristocracy of American fame and fortune, and was considered one of the most splendid and prestigious in all of the United States. Without asking if I was pleased with the hotel, my host registered me at the reception desk and escorted me to my room. Some room! It was a magnificent suite with extravagantly designed and stylized furnishings and every type of opulence, all of which looked like it belonged in a museum. During my many months in New York, before I joined Teddy Kollek in his suite in the Fourteen Hotel, which also doubled as the delegation's office, I had stayed in the Commodore Hotel on Forty-Second Street, where my room cost five dollars a night, including breakfast. This dream suite at the Beverly Wilshire made me uncomfortable and I felt completely out of my element.

After my host left, I asked the desk clerk for the price of the suite. It was twenty-five dollars a night, more than twice my allowance for board and lodging. While conversing with the clerk, I realized she was Jewish. I explained my problem to her, and she agreed to cancel my reservation and even ordered me a room in a commercial hotel in the city. I phoned my host and told him I was moving to another hotel. He was astonished, saying he'd intended to pay for my stay at the luxury hotel, but I told him I didn't think that was such a good idea. He had his own notions about the peculiarities of Israelis, which affected the way he saw my move. Over supper at his house, he introduced me to his wife, Shura, his son and his daughter, who were college students. They were a delightful family. Silk, his son, even invited a few of his friends from the university to hear from me firsthand about the war in Israel.

That same night, my host phoned the Mexican consul and made an appointment with him in his office in San Francisco. The next day, we flew together to San Francisco, and I had the opportunity to get to know him a lot better. What I saw was a man bursting with warmth, gregariousness, vast knowledge of the Russian classics, and a great love for Israel. Both he and his wife spoke fluent Russian, apparently their mother tongue, in which they spoke to each other. Their hobby was to compete as to who knew more Russian curses, a few of which were familiar to me, too. I thoroughly enjoyed those moments with him on the plane.

When we arrived in San Francisco and met with the Mexican consul in his office, he told us bad news: He had been instructed by his foreign minister to reject our request and not to approve my visa. The Mexican foreign minister was hostile to the State of Israel and had not been involved in our negotiations for the purchase of weapons. None of my host's attempts at persuasion did any good. The consul explained that his Foreign Ministry gave him no authority to grant a visa because of the war going on between Israel and the Arab armies. We continued to try and change his mind over lunch, but all in vain.

I reported the impasse to Kollek, suggesting that perhaps I should try flying to Mexico without a visa. He should contact Eli Sourasky, as well as Aryeh Dulzin, who was then resident in Mexico, asking them to meet me at the airport and to try and convince the authorities to allow me to enter Mexico. Kollek approved of the idea since there was really no other choice. I phoned Sourasky, gave him my flight number, and made sure he and Dulzin would be at the airport. I decided to fly with an American airline because a Mexican airline would more likely demand to see my passport and visa.

Sourasky and Dulzin met me at the airport's passport control desk and asked me to wait for the completion of the special arrangements they were making with the Interior Ministry and the airport authorities. After about half an hour, I was summoned to the counter where the passports were stamped, and the Mexican officer, who was in on the arrangements, handed me my visa and stamped my passport. On the ride from the airport, Sourasky told me he had put influential friends of his in the Interior Ministry to work and managed to convince them to instruct the Ministry's clerks at the airport to give me the visa.

Hank and Barbara Greenspan were waiting for me at the Reforma Hotel. He brought me up to date on the latest developments in the negotiations. Following the message I had sent him from Los Angeles, he informed the Mexican representatives that I was on my way and set up an appointment for me for the next morning at the Mexican Defense Ministry.

The arms we were negotiating for included fifty obsolete cannons, a large number of bombs, light arms, and a large quantity of ammunition for the cannons and for the other weapons, as well as American ammunition for 50-caliber machine guns. According to Greenspan, a Jewish major by the name of Miller of the American Artillery Corps had examined the cannons. He pronounced them in good working order and well maintained.

In conversation with the Mexican representatives I insisted that Greenspan and I visit the arsenal where the arms were stored, in order to see them for ourselves and so that I could give a description of the cannons to our purchasing people and Pinchas Sapir in Geneva. I took advantage of the opportunity to try my hand at bargaining, and I managed to get them to lower their price a little.

That same day I phoned Geneva. I reported to Sapir and Ginsburg on the progress of the negotiations, and on my impression of the high-ranking representatives of the Mexican army and government. Sapir and Ginsburg gave me a list of questions and demands connected with the procedures and with how the payment was to be transferred, and we agreed that I would enlist Eli Sourasky's help in planning the method of transmission.

Sourasky was the owner of the largest private bank in Mexico. It was agreed that the money would be deposited in his bank and would be made available and paid to my order. I reported this to Sapir and Ginsburg. Although they agreed to the arrangement, I didn't ask them to transfer the money, since the ship had not yet been purchased, and the fifty American tanks not yet released by the American authorities.

I brought Kollek up to date on the developments, and we agreed that he would send Rafael Recanati, who was in New York at the time, to purchase a ship in Canada. I have reason to believe that this first experience of Recanati's with the world of shipping played a role later in the Recanati concern's decision to establish a shipping company by the name of El-Yam.

Unfortunately, the delivery of the fifty new tanks, the core of the shipment, was held up by the United States State Department because of intelligence, or a suspicion, that the real end-user was not Mexico, as indicated in the export license, but Israel. Colonel Ives so informed his contact person Joe Buxenbaum, who served in the American Army with the rank of captain, adding that he hoped to overcome the problem and that the deal would go through. But Kollek and I had no faith in these promises. We knew that if there were any suspicion that Israel was involved in the deal, whether directly or indirectly, there was no power or trick that could coax the tanks from the American authorities. The American government enforced the embargo it had imposed on the export of arms and strategic materials to Israel. One can only imagine how the war might have proceeded if the tanks had reached the IDF during the second ceasefire.

Ives was holding a cash advance of $150,000, and we decided that when I returned from Mexico I would try to retrieve that sum from him. The Mexicans also received a considerable sum as an advance payment. Throughout our negotiations we never lost sight of that fact, which weighed heavily on our bargaining with them and made it hard for us to back away from the deal.

Rafael Recanati went to Canada where he purchased a ship named *Kafalos*, whose captain was Jewish. The ship's capacity was 10,000 tons; it was in reasonably good shape, and the price was right. As soon as Kollek gave me the schedule, I gave instructions to Sapir and Ginsburg to transfer the payment for it to Sourasky's bank.

In the meantime, President Alaman of Mexico received a telegram from Trygve Lie, the first Secretary-General of the United Nations, demanding that he should freeze the arms shipment. Fortunately, we hadn't paid any money yet; thus, we had a lever to pressure the Mexicans to let us go through with the loading. The Mexican representatives claimed they could not disobey the directives of the United Nations by loading the weapons, unless we could show them a final user document for any country other than Israel. We suggested that the weapons be loaded onto the ship and that it be placed under guard to prevent it from sailing until we presented them with the necessary document.

The Mexican arms and our arms cargo from the West Coast reached Tampico Bay. They were loaded onto the ship, where they were placed under guard of the Mexican army, which prevented its sailing. The news that a ship loaded with weapons bound for Israel was anchored in Tampico Bay was leaked to the Mexican press, which triggered a campaign of pressures by the large Arab population, among others, to keep the ship from going out to sea. We were racing against the clock, and we knew we had to get the necessary papers no matter what!

I don't remember whose idea it was to try and get official documents from the Chinese Embassy in Mexico City. It was probably

Hank Greenspan because he was always full of innovative ideas, and this idea had all the earmarks of Greenspan vintage. We knew the atmosphere at the Chinese embassy in Mexico City was one of panic and demoralization as a result of the great victories of the Communist army against the army of Nationalist China under Chiang Kai Shek, and we thought that in such a political climate, we might have a chance to achieve our objective. As we had hoped, when we visited the embassy we did succeed in paying to get some official forms, on which we typed the authorization that the shipment's destination was Nationalist China. Greenspan introduced himself as an arms merchant and me as the representative of one of the Arab states in the Persian Gulf, sent by its government to purchase arms.

This document satisfied the negotiators and enabled them to go through with the deal without fear of violating the orders of the United Nations Secretary-General. In order to conceal our cargo and to keep it from being discovered by the United Nations inspectors who had been stationed in Israel to supervise the ceasefires, we covered the weapons with two thousand tons of sugar, which was inexpensive in Mexico.

Before the ship set sail, Kollek sent two Israeli students to go along on the ship. One of them was a signalman, equipped with a radio; he maintained contact with Israel throughout the entire trip. I assigned the second escort to keep an eye on the ship's captain. His behavior and hints that we picked up from his wife, who was also on the boat, gave us the impression that he was not very stable.

As soon as the ship got underway, Sourasky transferred the payment for the arms to the Mexican government, in accordance with our agreement. News of the ship's sailing unleashed a storm among the heads of the Arab community in Mexico City and was given extensive coverage in the local newspapers. The Mexican representatives were afraid of losing control of the situation, and they asked Hank Greenspan and me to leave Mexico as quickly as possible. Sourasky, who was afraid of being adversely affected, backed up their request. I informed Kollek and we flew to New York.

The ship, which reached Israel during the second cease fire, passed the examinations of the United Nations inspectors. One anecdote that is deeply etched in my memory is the reception I was given by Eliezer Perry, who was in charge of food rations for the civilian population, when I returned upon completion of my mission in the United States. He embraced me and he told me he was happier about the arrival of the sugar than of the weapons because the country's store of sugar had run out without hope for another shipment during the next few weeks.

In contrast, the cannons, nicknamed the "Cucarachas" in the IDF, were delivered to the appropriate units, where they were received with mixed emotions due to their advanced age. However, at that point in the War of Independence, we couldn't afford to be picky.

During my visit at the Mexican arsenal, I saw a number of brand new 155-caliber American mountain cannons (Howitzers). After we stood firm and threatened to cancel the whole deal, I succeeded in getting two of these cannons from the Mexicans. They were the newest and most sophisticated artillery pieces that the IDF Artillery Corps had in those days.

Once the ship was unloaded, the *Kafalos* was transferred to the Zim Company, where its name was changed to *Dromit*, and it became the first ship owned by the company.

I must stress that Eli Sourasky was a central participant in this operation, who took considerable risks upon himself. The deal could not have been made without him. Years later, Sourasky funded Sourasky Garden near the Habima Theater, and he donated over ten million dollars for the erection of Ichilov Hospital, which today goes by his name, the Tel Aviv Sourasky Medical Center. His ties with us—with Kollek and with me—continued after the war, and we would meet on his many visits to Israel. On one of those visits, Kollek arranged a fascinating tour of the excavations in the Old City of Jerusalem for Sourasky and me, and our wives.

Hank Greenspan, his wife Barbara, and their children in the Nevada desert

The Critical Importance of the Arms Shipments on the Eve of the War of Independence and During the War

Airlifts in the first Balak operations, the ships *Nora* and *Shayo* from Czechoslovakia, and many other vessels that arrived during the course of the war, brought weapons that constituted the primary source for the arming of the Haganah and the Palmach in the months that preceded the establishment of the state and, after 1948, of the IDF units. These deliveries went a long way toward bridging the huge gap in the early stages of the war between what we needed for our necessities on the one hand, and the scant number of weapons that the combat units had at their disposal, on the other. One of many possible illustrations of this gap is the fact that the battalion commanded at that time by Yitzhak Pundak, which numbered eight hundred fighters, was equipped with only four hundred rifles when it was sent to reinforce the Negev Brigade. And that was not the only time fighters were forced to take turns using available weapons.

In all probability, many months before the declaration of the state, we could have brought a considerable quantity of cannons of various calibers, fighter planes, and disassembled armored personnel carriers, packed and concealed, using the same method by which we brought the shipments of equipment, machinery, strategic materials, explosives, and a significant quantity of weapons from the United States and Italy. I am not including tanks in this appraisal, since a tank is a huge, heavy mass, nearly impossible to disassemble and camouflage.

There's no question that had that happened, the war would have taken a different course. It would have been shorter and we might have been spared difficult and painful episodes such as the fall of the Etzion Bloc, the slaughter of the Thirty-Five, the Arab Legion's conquest of the Old City, the many casualties of the failed battles at Latrun, the need to create the Burma Road, and the siege of Jerusalem, the murder of the convoy of doctors and nurses on the way to Hadassah Hospital on Mount Scopus, the many casualties of the Yechiam convoy, the cutting off of the Negev from the center of the country, and the evacuation of the settlements that could not withstand the land attacks and the bombardment from air by the Egyptian and Syrian armies.

There's no doubt that the attacks on the Iraqi es-Suweidan police fortress which were failures and cost us many lives, could have been prevented, and we could have taken the Egyptian forces cut off at the Faluja Pocket captive, together with their commander, the daring Sudanese Brigadier Taha and Gamal Abdel Nasser, who was one of his officers.

It is even possible that the War of Independence might have developed along lines similar to those of the future Six Day War, with all the political, military, and demographic ramifications that would have entailed. I'm basing this conjecture on the fact that, during the War of Independence, even without artillery worthy of the name and without a meaningful air force, in Operation Horev IDF units in the Negev under the command of Yigal Allon, commander of the southern front, succeeded in cutting off the Egyptian army from its base and from its supply lines in Egypt.

The IDF was forced to withdraw from the approaches to El Arish because of the tremendous pressure and threats by the British and American governments and other international bodies. Before the withdrawal, Allon tried to convince Ben-Gurion to retain the conquered territories in the Sinai so as to force the High Command of the Egyptian army and the Egyptian government to sign a peace treaty with Israel, but Allon's efforts failed when Britain threatened to wage war on the IDF forces if they did not withdraw from the Sinai. In fact, what developed was a strategic situation that was similar, if not identical, to the encirclement of the Third army in the Yom Kippur War.

I find it necessary to mention this because I am aware of conflicting versions put forward by historians, commentators, and various researchers, and of their tendency to blame the leadership, first and foremost Ben-Gurion, for shortsightedness and for not having the daring to equip our forces with artillery and fighter planes, which could have been brought in as camouflaged shipments several months before the war. But to the best of my knowledge, there is no justification for this view since the initiatives, the ideas, the location of sources and of ways to execute plans, had always come from the purchasing people, including myself.

Apparently, we lacked the vision, the creative imagination, and the foresight to take the initiative to bring these programs to the attention of our leadership, even though after World War II there were great surpluses of weapons, which were accessible. I can say in my own defense that my main preoccupation, together with that of Slavin, was the development of our military industry, and establishing it as a modern and extensive industry, capable of coping with the many challenges with which it was faced in those fateful days. My activity in arms procurement was in the form of sorties, at my own initiative, in which I carried out operations assigned to me by the National High Command, before whom I had presented my ideas.

Nevertheless, it may well be that the responsibility for the failure was indeed mine, since it was I who took the initiative and paved the way for the resumption of arms shipments from across the ocean after the World War, and who built the infrastructure and the system for the shipment of the machinery, equipment, and strategic materials from the United States as well as the first weapons deliveries from Europe.

How many times have I tortured myself that I didn't make the Haganah High Command, and particularly the chief of the Haganah and Ben-Gurion, aware as early as 1947 of the possibility of bringing heavy weapons and disassembled and concealed fighter planes, just as we brought scores of shipments from the United States and the arms accumulated in Italy from Jewish soldiers and officers. Without a doubt, had Eliyahu Golomb been alive during those years, our procurement activity would have burst out of its bonds and included efforts to bring those more creative types of arms as well.

The children of some of the members of the IDF mission in Prague, including also the author's daughters

David Ben-Gurion

David Ben-Gurion was blessed with exceptional curiosity and a great love for science. He was captivated by the mystery surrounding the human brain, and he had many discussions about this field of human endeavor and other subjects with the senior scientists of his time who had close relations with him and were often invited to his home. This was a group of scientists from among the most highly respected in scientific research in Israel, including Ernst Hugo Bergman, Efraim and Aharon Katzir (Efraim Katzir later served as Israel's fourth president), Amos DeShalit, Professor Rakach, Professor Farkash, and Haim Sheba. These were received like members of the family in Ben-Gurion's office and home, and he would question them about every detail in the various areas of science. His attraction to science, however, was matched by his love for ancient Greek philosophy and literature.

In one of the meetings between Ben-Gurion, Slavin, and me, in which we planned to discuss with him our agenda for the period ahead, he greeted us with an erudite lecture on the supreme necessity of learning all there was to learn about the construction and development of advanced, smart weapons and the intensive and extensive development of scientific research in general. He elucidated on the geo-strategic background of our region, so fraught with dangers and threats to the existence of our people that it obliged us to equip ourselves with these types of weapons.

This idea was evidently born from his discussions with the group of scientists, and to this end he decided to establish Hemed, the acronym for "Science Corps" in Hebrew, to be headed by Shlomo Gur (Grazovsky), the planner of the buildings and fortifications of the Homa Umigdal (Wall and Watchtower) settlements. Hemed was the nucleus from which, following the War of Independence, the Rafael industries grew.

One of Ben-Gurion's claims was that Jewish genius was capable of developing sophisticated weapons systems which would be an aid in the all-round security of the state. He believed with all his heart that our Israeli scientists, with the help of other Jewish scientists, had the potential to plan and to build these types of weapons.

Though Slavin was vigorously opposed to the decision to establish Hemed, he held his tongue until Ben-Gurion finished speaking. Then he could no longer contain himself. His emotional and skeptical response was quickly forthcoming, and he rejected the idea, claiming that Ben-Gurion was no expert or engineer and was not equipped with the knowledge necessary to establish a project like Hemed. He added that Ben-Gurion lacked the requisite professional tools to weigh and initiate such a program. "The Old Man," who appreciated Slavin's technical, organizational, and planning talents and abilities despite the latter's uncontrolled temperament, was unruffled by the outburst and refrained from ejecting us unceremoniously. Silence hung in the air for a few moments. Then Ben-Gurion said calmly, "You're right that I am not an engineer or a scientist, but I'm entitled to consider myself an engineer of engineers."

As a matter of fact, Ben-Gurion was correct, since Churchill, Roosevelt, Truman, and Stalin were not scientists or engineers either. And there can be no doubt that, like them, Ben-Gurion was the kind of leader who comes along once in a century—in his intellectual and spiritual stature, in his ability to penetrate the intricacies of military and strategic issues, in his gift for leadership and his vision, and in his ability to lead the people in the crucial hours in which their destiny was being determined. After his conversation with Slavin, his incisive pronouncement that he was "an engineer's engineer" was retold again and again. I, too, had a hand in publicizing it.

As for Slavin, not many people knew him as well as I did, and I can testify unequivocally that his was an unrivaled genius for seeing the whole picture and for planning projects, translating them into their component parts, and implementing them while creating a great momentum that could sweep along with it all who worked with him.

To the best of my understanding, Slavin's resistance to the establishment of Hemed resulted from his mistaken idea that all weapons development activities should be a part of Ta'as. After the establishment of Hemed, I had many conversations with Shlomo Gur on this topic, and I managed to convince Slavin of the justification for the existence of an independent organization working to develop advanced, precise, sophisticated types of weapons, and harnessing the best engineering and scientific minds to these undertakings. The role of Ta'as, in contrast, would be to apply these inventions and to engage in the production of weapons based on orders placed by the IDF. I was the bridge between Ta'as and Hemed.

Our conversation with Ben-Gurion took place in mid-1948. We were both amazed at Ben-Gurion's vision, but we quickly learned to appreciate the scope of his thought and his far-reaching vision. As we walked out of the meeting, I said to Slavin that, metaphorically, Ben-Gurion's ideas were similar to a trouserless man dreaming of buying a top hat. But one had to admire his ability to see well beyond the horizon, which far exceeded what any other mere mortal could discern. Slavin responded that he agreed, but only with the first half of my metaphor.

These descriptions may seem trivial, but they reveal and give resonance to the atmosphere of that period. Perhaps it is to that atmosphere that I ascribe the sadness I feel every year on Israel Independence Day, a day when I cannot manage to rid myself of my melancholy and I wonder whatever became of the vision, values, and heritage that the "founding fathers" entrusted into the hands of our generation.

To our great misfortune, all that we see today is the complete opposite of the lofty aspirations that characterized those days: a total lack of vision, a new reality of "eat, drink, and be merry," a race after material attainments which have become the supreme value and the essence of life, enormous social gaps, and the downgrading of the teachings and the ideological, social, ethical, and human values which bore our founding generations on their wings.

Production of a Prototype
of a 120-Caliber Mortar

In early 1949, Slavin went abroad to purchase machinery and equipment, and to obtain advice and know-how from various factories about how to set up a plant for the production of cannonballs. We felt that this was a once-in-a-lifetime opportunity to expand the current production of light arms and ammunition (mortars, submachine guns, "Dror" light machine guns, light ammunition, etc.) to the manufacture of cannonballs. In a high-level discussion with the minister of defense and director general of the ministry, Pinhas Sapir, a plan was outlined and approved for our own independent production of heavy arms with an initial budget of $1 million to pay for purchases necessary to carry out the first phase of the program. Later, additional funds would be needed to complete the acquisition of the equipment, and we would face the problem of getting a budget to erect the large construction needed to establish and implement the project.

After the British evacuated the country, the Quartermaster-General Branch GHQ seized the large center for storage as well as the warehouses in Tira, and it occurred to me that one of the large buildings could be suitable as a production hall for this plant.

Major General Avidar, then head of the Quartermaster Branch, opposed the idea, asserting that his branch was the official and natural body to take charge of any buildings, workshops, and other facilities available in the center of the country.

In order to stake out our claim to possession of the building, I decided to make our right to the building an established fact, and I gave my assistant at that time, Yosef Yariv, the job of organizing a unit of Ta'as employees to seize the building and occupy it. When Avidar heard about this, he ordered Brigadier Asher Peled, commander of the Ordnance Corps, to keep us from claiming control of the building.

We were determined in our resistance, and I suggested turning the dispute over to Yaakov Dori, chief of General Staff of the IDF to study and render his decision. After Avidar and I each presented our cases, Dori decided to designate the building for the establishment of the shell factory. Now we could assemble the equipment right away and proceed with production almost immediately. The problem of finances, which posed great difficulties and delayed the operation for a long time, was thus solved to the satisfaction of the director-general of the Ministry of Defense, Pinhas Sapir, and of the Ta'as people.

In the absence of the general manager, one day I was summoned to a meeting in the office of the minister of defense, Ben-Gurion, in my capacity as acting manager of Ta'as. Present at the meeting were the minister of defense, Chief of General Staff Dori, head of the Operations Branch in the General Staff Yigal Yadin, head of the Quartermaster Branch Avidar, and the military secretary of the minister of defense, Colonel Nehemia Argov. Yigal Yadin presented the subject for discussion: the urgent need to develop a weapons system that would be capable of "cracking open" fortified bunkers. It had become clear that some battles did not end successfully because the IDF lacked a weapon that could penetrate bunkers and fortified buildings in which enemy units were entrenched. The heavy mortars that had arrived in shipments from abroad were not up to the task.

In the discussion a proposal was made to produce a heavy mortar, capable of firing heavy shells containing a large quantity of explosives, based on the assumption that the weight of the shell together with the force of the explosion would shatter the fortified structures. When it became clear that shells from an 81-caliber mortar were not suitable for such a job, I suggested producing a 120-caliber mortar and especially powerful shells, even if this had an effect on the range. Ben-Gurion was keenly interested in the idea. The project was approved and Ta'as was given a special budget to finance the construction of a prototype which would be an exact copy of a foreign-made mortar.

In the discussion, Ben-Gurion expressed his desire to personally take part in the testing of the prototype when it was ready. I was asked to outline a timetable, and I specified a period of two to three months. Following the discussion, this project was placed at the head of the list of priorities of the planning department of Ta'as. Headed by the engineers Blau and Weiler, our team began working feverishly according to the guidelines, data, and specifications of the General Staff.

As I have said, a foreign-made mortar was chosen as the model to be imitated. To produce the barrel for the prototype, we needed a thick-walled pipe that would be able to withstand the tremendous pressure that the firing would create. A great deal of experience had been accumulated at Ta'as in the manufacture of barrels from thick rolls of highly flexible tin with a special metallurgical composition, which were then rounded to form pipes, using the same process developed for the manufacture of the barrels of the 52- and 81-caliber mortars. The barrel of the 120-caliber mortar would also be produced using the same process, from tin rolls each weighing more than a ton each. A large amount of this tin was "procured" from the warehouses of the British Fleet in Haifa Port during World

War II, with the help of a Jew who worked in the warehouses, and by means of forged authorizations and forms (using the "arms train" method), in an operation that I planned and implemented.

I assigned the management of the mortar project to Yaakov Lior, one of the pillars of Ta'as, and an outstanding expert. He had rich professional experience, organizational ability, and extensive technical knowledge. He was the head of Maflan, one of the sections of the central plant of Ta'as, which also housed the top management offices.

Planning and production of the shells and fuses was assigned to another section head, Isser Snapiry, who had amassed extensive technical know-how, excelled in his creative imagination, and who had always shown a gift for improvising.

The construction of the prototype and the production of several dozen shells were completed on time, and in consultation with the minister of defense. We set May 16, 1949 as the date for testing. We chose a strip of the coast in Jaffa, in the Ajami area, for the test site, with the firing to be targeted to the south (what was to become the Bat Yam Shooting Range).

In the area where the shells were expected to fall, we built a fortified trench on the side of a hill bordering the beach, for the safety of the invited guests and observers from the General Staff. From this point the minister of defense, the chief of General Staff, Golda Meir, and several major generals from the General Staff were to observe the landing of the shells. In the course of the test it turned out that the choice of that spot for the protective installation was calculated correctly (six or seven kilometers from the firing point), since a number of shells fell a few dozen meters from the fortified position. Ben-Gurion, fearless and inclined to take risks, stood erect in order to see the shells landing, and I had to grab his vest and pull him back into the trench.

The test in its entirety was crowned with success. The shells reached the planned distances and all of them exploded and left a crater of a diameter and depth that testified to the force of the explosion and destruction. The mortar with all its parts passed all the tests and parameters that had been set for it, and the system's performance was a match for the mortar we had copied. The shells were our own creation, different in several components from the foreign model. They were designed according to the requirements of the General Staff, to intensify their destructive force.

In advance coordination with the office of the minister of defense, we decided to take advantage of the presence of the minister of defense, the chief of General Staff and several of its major generals, Golda Meir, Teddy Kollek, and other invited guests to give a live demonstration of the types of weapons produced by Ta'as: 52-, 81-, and 120-caliber mortars, a few models of the "Dror" light machine gun, Sten submachine guns, launchers for rifle grenades, light ammunition of different calibers, hand grenades, and others. The event lasted the entire day. It went smoothly and according to the timetable we had planned, and it won the praise of the minister of defense and all present. An employee of Ta'as photographed every stage of the test without my knowledge; that series of pictures was also sent to the honored guests. After the test, Ben-Gurion praised Ta'as' central role in bridging the enormous gap between our security needs and the weapons at the disposal of the Haganah units and the Jewish settlements during the Arab Revolt, of the escorts of the convoys to besieged Jerusalem during the War of Independence, and of the IDF, until the arms shipments began to arrive from Italy, Czechoslovakia, and other countries.

The weapons produced by Ta'as and the arms shipments from abroad made it possible for the Jewish Yishuv to defend itself against the Arab forces. When weapons production expanded and shipments of combat equipment, including fighter planes and bombers, began flowing in from abroad, the IDF was in possession of the tools it needed for major offensives and for the defeat of the Arab armies.

It was not without reason that Ben-Gurion wrote in a letter to me on April 3, 1949: "I ask you to give the thanks of the government to the management and all the employees [at Ta'as] for their dedication and diligence. Their share in our victories is no less than the share of the army, and the advanced work and management skill of our production plants is a source of great pride."

מדינת ישראל
הממשלה הזמנית
לשכת ראש הממשלה

1369

הקריה, ד' ניסן תש"ט
3.4.49

לא. סחרוב – סגן–אלוף
מפעלים לייצור נשק.

אני סאסר בתודה את קבלת התרשומת
על תפוקת הכדורים. התקדמות המפעל מצודדת
ומשמחת, ואבקשך למסור הוקרת הממשלה להנהלה
ולכל הפועלים על מסירותם וחריצותם – חלקם
בנצחונותינו אינו פחות מחלקו של הצבא, ויש
להתגאות על כושר העבודה וההנהלה המתקדמה של
מפעלי הייצור שלנו.

חזון ואמצו.

ד. בן–גוריון
ראש הממשלה ושר הבטחון

Letter from Prime Minister and Minister of Defense, David Ben-Gurion to the author, praising his work with the Ammunition Plant, April 3, 1949

Ben-Gurion and Golda Meir attend the testing of a new 120 mm mortar produced by Ta'as (Military Industries)

The author during a conversation with Mrs. Golda Meir

At the "mortar demonstration" held at the Bat Yam Shooting Range in May 1949, the leadership were also shown other weapons developed at Ta'as

The Crisis Surrounding the Appointment of Haim Bar-Lev as Chief of Staff

A few weeks before the Six Day War broke out, I was about to leave for Europe on a business trip with my wife. I took my leave of Yigal Allon, Israel Galili, and Colonel Yosef Yariv (a Palmach veteran and a senior member of the Mossad), who asked me to meet with Haim Bar-Lev in Paris. I was to tell him they were making every effort to ensure his appointment as chief of staff after Yitzhak Rabin concluded his term of service in the spirit of an agreement made before Bar-Lev had left Israel.

Before Haim Bar-Lev left for France, he had served as the head of the Operations Branch at the General Staff, and Major-General Ezer Weizmann replaced him in that post for a period of a year. The decision as to which of the two was to be appointed chief of staff would be made close to the end of Rabin's term of office. These unexpected reversals were very upsetting to Bar-Lev, calling into question the appointment that he had been so sure of. He was advised to use the year to study in Paris, and to await Eshkol's decision when the time came. Bitterly, he decided to retire from the army, even drafting a letter of resignation. When Yigal Allon, Galili, and other friends learned about this, they asked him to come to the roof of Yariv's house for a discussion.

This conversation with his close friends, including Dado (David Eleazar), was stormy and protracted, since Bar-Lev had made up his mind to submit his letter of resignation. His friends urged him not to take a hasty step, but rather to act on the suggestion of a year's study in France. They pointed out that once he submitted his resignation he wouldn't be able to turn back, and they wanted him to give them time to try and intervene with Eshkol on his behalf. He relented on his decision to resign only after his friends promised him they would be vigilant, to prevent the creation of a *fait accompli* in the appointment of Weizmann.

When I arrived in Paris, I met with Bar-Lev in Café de Lappé and told him about my conversations with Galili, Allon, and Yariv and the message they'd asked me to deliver to him. Bar-Lev was bitterly disappointed with the way things were going. He had already been in Paris for several months and had a sinking feeling that the die was already cast, and that he was sitting there in vain, far from where all the decisions were being made.

Our conversation continued for several hours. I tried to persuade him to wait a few more weeks, to give me time to report to his friends about how he was feeling and about his inclination to go back home. I promised him that on my return to Israel I would meet personally with Eshkol to try to get a sense of "which way the wind was blowing." I would then give him a report about this conversation. Bar-Lev finally agreed to my suggestion—though doing so caused him great torment—and we agreed to meet and speak again before I left for home.

Towards morning the next day, the phone rang in my hotel room at the Hotel Continental. It was Bar-Lev, to tell me that the day before there had been a dogfight with the Syrian air force, in which we had downed seven Syrian planes, without our suffering any losses. I felt that ominous clouds were gathering on the horizon and decided to cancel a pleasure trip I'd planned to take with my wife to Brittany and returned home.

As soon as I arrived, I met with Allon, Galili, and Yariv, and we agreed to make another effort on Bar-Lev's behalf, as I had promised. Galili and Allon said they had had discussions with Eshkol but hadn't managed to get an unequivocal answer as to whether he'd made up his mind about Bar-Lev's appointment. They were aware of my friendship with Eshkol and suggested that I make an appointment with him and report to him about my discussions with Bar-Lev, and try to get an idea what his inclination was. That is what I had planned to do anyway, but I decided that first it would be a good idea to speak with Golda Meir, who was then secretary of the alignment of Labor parties, and win her over to our joint effort.

I was surprised to learn that Meir had never met Bar-Lev. In the course of our discussion, she told me of the relationship of admiration and friendship that had developed between her and Yitzhak Rabin, whose reliability and whose sense of responsibility as chief of staff had impressed her greatly. Meir said this friendship had special significance for her, against the background of some bitter experiences she had had with Moshe Dayan and others in the defense establishment during her term of office as foreign minister. I took advantage of the praise she lavished on Rabin, and I described Bar-Lev to her as a gifted military man with a great deal of experience and many achievements to his credit, similar to Yitzhak Rabin in his honesty, reliability, and steadfastness. I judged that these qualities gave him an advantage over Major General Ezer Weizmann, who had a reputation for being impulsive, impatient, quick-tempered, and lacking in skills of deliberation.

Meir agreed to my request that she talk about Bar-Lev's appointment with Eshkol at the first opportunity, advising me to meet with him as well. And so it was that after Meir spoke with Eshkol,

I met with him. I told him about my conversations with Bar-Lev and his frame of mind, and described, as I had to Meir, what we thought were the points in his favor in the contest for the position of chief of staff.

Eshkol was furious at the insufferable pressure being exerted on him by several people on behalf of both of the candidates, and blamed me for being among the spokesmen striving to get Bar-Lev appointed. Nevertheless, I had the impression, in the course of our discussion, that the balance was beginning to tilt in Bar-Lev's favor, although Eshkol said nothing specific.

This conversation took place shortly before Independence Day 1967. When Egyptian military forces started to stream into the Sinai and clouds of war were forming on the horizon, Bar-Lev was called back home. After so much time has passed, it's hard to judge how much influence the pressure applied by Bar-Lev's supporters had on the cabinet's decision to bring him back to Israel and appoint him deputy chief of staff. At any rate, the fact is that Minister of Defense Moshe Dayan was determined that Bar-Lev become chief of staff. He said this to Bar-Lev as soon as the battles of the Six Day War were over.

When Bar-Lev was appointed chief of staff after the war, I arranged a meeting between him and Amnon Rubinstein, founder and head of the Shinui party, and they conducted a dialogue that went on for quite awhile in meetings at my house. This was the first opportunity Bar-Lev had to learn about the social and political issues that were then on the public agenda.

The Appointment of Haim Bar-On as Yigal Allon's Personal Assistant and Bureau Chief

---

One day in the early 1970s, when Yigal Allon was serving as minister of education and filling in for Prime Minister Golda Meir while she was abroad, he pulled me out of a meeting of the board of directors of a plant of which I was the general manager and asked me to recommend one or more candidates for the job of his bureau chief and personal assistant. He stressed that this was very urgent because of the tremendous workload in his office. Of course I acceded to his request and promised to find him someone as quickly as possible.

Pondering the matter, I recalled that my daughter Naomi had told me that her husband, David Kolitz, had a childhood friend named Haim Bar-On who had returned to Israel after four years of university studies in England. I spoke with my son-in-law, telling him of Allon's request, and asking him to describe his friend's personality, talents, and character in greater detail. I also asked David if he thought Bar-On possessed the qualities that would make him suitable for such a job. David asked me to give him a few days to think about it. In the same conversation, he told me that on previous occasions Bar-On had expressed his profound admiration for

Allon's personality and social and political views, and that he even went so far as to say it was his life's dream to work with him.

After a few days, David told me that, after careful consideration, he had come to the conclusion that Haim's characteristics, education, and social background suited the requirements of the position, and that he was well up to the task. Furthermore, he had conversed with Bar-On to "feel him out" and was impressed by his eagerness to get the job.

I described the man to Allon and he approved and gave me the green light to talk to Bar-On and offer him the job. We agreed that I would invite him to my house, while Allon would send Eliyahu Chassin, his political advisor, to also consider him.

We met with Bar-On at my home and, after a lengthy conversation and "cross examination," we concluded that he had the background and qualifications for the job. And indeed, Haim Bar-On, who was appointed to the position, quickly became Yigal Allon's right hand man and confidant, recognized as such by the political and party establishment, and was his acknowledged loyal representative before the public bodies and individuals with whom Allon had contact. For Bar-On this was not just a job but a calling, and he was an active participant in Allon's many meetings as minister of education and as foreign minister, always at his side, until Allon's premature death in 1980.

Yigal Allon's sudden death, which stunned all his many friends and admirers, was for Bar-On an unbearable blow, to the point that he felt himself orphaned. From that point on he dedicated himself to the preservation of Allon's legacy. He even named his daughter Alona.

The 1977 elections brought about a great upheaval in Israel's government—the Likud took the reins and the Ma'arach (Alignment—the result of the merging of Mapai—the Israel Labor Party—with the United Labor Party as well as the Rafi Party in Israel) became the opposition. Haim Bar-On decided to retire from public service and to turn to the business world. After trying his hand at various endeavors, he chose to focus on communications and publishing. He was very successful and founded one periodical after another, such as *Monitin* and *Globes*. He built up a career full of accomplishments, and his fine reputation placed him at the forefront of Israel's publishing houses and print and broadcast media. He gave the editors of his periodicals autonomy and support, and to editors who won his trust he gave the space to maneuver that enabled them to display their knowledge and their journalistic perspective. He studiously avoided using his newspapers as advertising tools for his personal opinions, and he never sought headlines for himself.

Bar-On was a man of principles and of solid political and social views, enterprising and dynamic. Towards the end of his life he invested in the newspaper *Yediot Aharonot*, together with Eliezer Fishman. He was outgoing and a loyal friend, and was known for his generosity, always ready to lend a hand to friends in need.

Yossi Chechanover, Chairman of the Board of Directors of El Al, who was an intimate friend of Moshe Dayan's and the legal advisor for the ministry of defense, heaped praises on Haim Bar-On in a letter he wrote to me. He noted especially the bond and the cooperation between him and Bar-On in passing messages and otherwise acting as liaisons between Moshe Dayan and Yigal Allon, whose complex relationship kept them from having direct contact with each other during certain periods.

Earlier, Haim Yisraeli and I also made a similar attempt to mediate between the two, but our effort was not very successful.

Golda Meir

The turning point of the Yom Kippur War came after the IDF crossed the Suez Canal, with the help of the large quantity of weapons that started to pour in by airlift from the United States on giant Galaxy (c-5A) planes. This materiel made up for the heavy losses in weapons, equipment, and aircraft inflicted on the IDF in the initial stages of the war. Anyone who followed the course of events of that time knows about the political and bureaucratic obstacles that thwarted all the initial efforts in this operation. It was only when that outstanding personality, Golda Meir, stepped in and won over Nixon and Kissinger with her powers of persuasion and her forcefulness that the hindrances—the bureaucrats and the "not-so-bureaucrats" that stood in the way of launching the airlift—were swept aside.

I cannot resist expressing my admiration for that great woman. I can see it all now: her steadfastness, and that of Chief of General Staff David Eleazar, who shouldered the burden of the horrors and the fears of those terrible days without flinching. The senior officers of the IDF were also greatly encouraged by the support and backing she gave them. It should be remembered that, at that moment in time, others of our leaders felt as if the world was caving in, became dejected, and not a few of them panicked.

But that wasn't all. As one who was deeply involved with arms procurement of desperately needed equipment for the combat units on the eve of the War of Independence and in its initial stages, I am taking the liberty of stating that I believe Meir deserves to be considered the true hero of that war, second only to Ben-Gurion. In setting out on a trip to raise money for arms purchases in Czechoslovakia and other lands, she won her way into the hearts of American Jews and moved them to provide the IDF and the Israeli government with the huge sums of money needed to pay for the war.

While I was in the United States, I had the opportunity to follow Meir's activities. I was witness to the efforts she invested, her zeal, persistence, and persuasiveness, which were evident in her contacts with Jewish communities and individuals, as she traveled the length and the breadth of the United States. She succeeded in giving large segments of American Jewry the sense of a shared fate with the Jewish Yishuv fighting for its life. It is impossible to comprehend the extensive purchasing enterprise in Europe and the United States and the financing of the needs of war without realizing the crucial role she played. There is no way the IDF could have stemmed the flood of Arab armies—not to mention defeating them—during the War of Independence, equipped only with sub-machine guns, a small number of machine guns and mortars, and insufficient quantity of rifles, some of which were museum pieces! The sum total of weapons the IDF had when it was getting organized was a mere nine thousand rifles, a small number of 2- and 3-inch mortars, and a few Sten submachine guns.

I'm aware that what I say is not popular and it's no great pleasure to swim against the current, but I feel I have an obligation to reject with all my heart the defamation and the smear campaign waged against Golda Meir when she was prime minister. I also reject the charge that she was responsible for ignoring Anwar Sadat's hints and signals concerning his willingness to negotiate a resolution to the conflict with Israel before the outbreak of the Yom Kippur War. It can't be denied that, as prime minister, she was responsible for the failure of her government on the eve of that war, and she never tried to shrug off that responsibility. But I have it on good authority that there was verified information in the hands of the pertinent members of the government that there was no real, serious intention behind Sadat's hints and signals, and that they were simply intended as a diversion.

Meir was not unreasonably stubborn in her rejection of a change in status quo on the Egyptian front or of a proposal that she act as if she were agreeing to admitting armed Egyptian forces on the eastern bank of the Canal, since in December 1971, after clarifications received from the United States, Israel had agreed to far-reaching concessions on the following issues: the IDF's withdrawal in Sinai as far as the Passes; an Egyptian armed presence on the east bank of the Canal; and acceptance of all parts of UN Resolution 242.

These concessions were not long in coming. We know this from Sadat himself, in an interview reported in *Newsweek*, when he said he was prepared to move forward toward a resolution.*

But the truth is, Sadat was not interested in the details of an arrangement for the opening of the Canal, but only in an Israeli commitment to pull back from all the territories, on all our borders, including a withdrawal from East Jerusalem, according to a pre-agreed timetable. For this we can rely on Kissinger's testimony in his book, *The White House Years.*

In March 1973 (six months before the Yom Kippur War), Golda Meir authorized Henry Kissinger to inform Sadat of Israel's agreement to a settlement according to the formula "sovereignty in

* December 13, 1971.

exchange for security," meaning the return of the entire Sinai to Egyptian sovereignty in exchange for a solution of Israel's security problems in Sinai, using modest means.

But Sadat absolutely rejected this American-Israeli offer in a speech he made on March 26, 1973, in a joint session of the Egyptian People's Council and the Central Committee of the Arab Socialist Union. In other words, in the early 1970s Sadat was not accepting of any settlement with Israel on the Israeli-Egyptian border alone.

The accusation that Meir passed up opportunities to make peace is likewise specious. Diplomatic documents available to us today—and of special importance, American documents—prove that Sadat was not prepared to agree to any settlement at all, however partial, temporary, or minimalist, unless Israel committed itself in advance to a withdrawal from all the territories, and not only from Sinai. The government could not possibly have agreed to such a withdrawal, and it seems to me that this was the policy of subsequent governments, as well.

In taking Meir's measure, we mustn't forget this fateful decision, which mitigates to some extent the dreadful blunder of not calling up the reserves earlier and preparing for war in time. In its first partial report, even the Agranat Commission, which investigated the surprise attack of the Yom Kippur War, found that the prime minister had decided quickly and wisely, following healthy instincts, in favor of mobilization of our entire reserves system and thereby did what was most important in saving the country.

There is no justification for the charge that Meir, of all people, should have detected the clouds of war gathering on the horizon. It was also unrealistic to demand of her profound military insight, when there were battle-tested chiefs of staff with rich military experience serving in her government. It is only logical to see these people as being truly responsible for our having been caught by surprise, for our army's unpreparedness at the outbreak of the Yom Kippur War, and for the "total eclipse" in the first stages of the war.

Furthermore, one must not forget that on the day the war broke out, on Saturday, October 6, Meir settled the dispute between Chief of Staff David Eleazar and Minister of Defense Moshe Dayan on the question of calling up the reserves. Dayan thought it would be enough to call up a limited number of some fifty to sixty thousand soldiers, comprising two divisions, whereas Eleazar demanded Dayan's authorization to induct two hundred thousand reservists, the sum total of all combat formations.

After the two men stated their cases, Meir decided in favor of pulling in all the reserves. Dado's explanation convinced her that the reserves could be deployed immediately, so that on Sunday morning they would be able to go to battle, whereas reserves not assembled now wouldn't be able to participate in the fateful initial stages of the war. And indeed, the reserve forces whose call-up was in dispute played a decisive role in the October 7 battles to halt the enemy's advance and on the northern front at least, the advance would not have been contained without them.

The 146th Division, the reserves of the General Staff, which was inducted on Saturday as part of Dado's recommendation, was the only force which reported, at the last minute, opposite Syrian tanks and columns that had succeeded in penetrating the Golan Heights and were advancing on the southern axis heading toward Lake Kinneret. The way was almost completely open before them because of the lack of manpower to stop them. It isn't hard to imagine how serious the situation would have been if this force had not been sent to the front on Saturday morning and if their joining the battle had been delayed by a day.

Even though I have described above the events of but a single day, it was a fateful day, thanks to which the IDF succeeded in halting Syria's assault and repelling its armored columns from the territories it had conquered. We even gained a hold on Syrian and Egyptian territory in counterattacks, despite our disastrous situation at the outbreak of the war. The sudden Egyptian and Syrian attack was reminiscent of the German army's surprise invasion of Poland and Russia in World War II, when the latter were caught totally unprepared to fight back.

Indeed, Golda Meir won her place in the sun with her historic decision.

Let us not forget that these achievements of the IDF brought about the collapse of the Khartoum Conference's three "no's"—"No peace, no negotiations, and no recognition"—the iron-clad principle that there would be no negotiating with Israel until it agreed to an all-out withdrawal from all of the occupied territories and a solution to the Palestinian problem. They also cleared the way for Egypt's separate peace with Israel.

The authority bestowed on the Agranat Commission in its letter of appointment to investigate the first three days of the war only, and the parts of their report that were made public were responsible in no small measure, in my opinion, for the assertion by the Arab nations that it was they who had won the war—a legend that indoctrinated their people with a distorted picture of the war.

Ironically, the picture of the Yom Kippur War is perceived, even among parts of the Israeli public, as one of defeat, because the investigation of the war concentrated only on the stages in which there were many shortcomings, leaving large segments of the population with the impression that the whole war was a failure.

It is hard for me to understand how two former chiefs of staff could have agreed to serve on a commission whose jurisdiction was limited to a format so illogical and unjust as to create a distorted and misleading picture of the war as one integral whole. This was a great injustice to more than a few of the officers who participated in that war, and first and foremost to Chief of Staff David Elazar, who proved his mastery, command, steadfastness, determined military leadership, and profound understanding of strategy in his conduct of the war. It is hard to understand how military men, of all people, did not utilize their specific military expertise in cabinet deliberations and demand the call-up of the reserves in time to prevent the "surprise."

In appraising Golda Meir's functioning as prime minister, one must take into account the force of her personality, her great influence on world leaders (and particularly on those of the United States), and her having been, in my opinion, the most brilliant spokesperson and advocate that the state has seen since its founding. We remember her persuasiveness and the power of her belief in her proud appearances before world leaders and in press conferences in which the greatest journalists and analysts listened reverently, sitting before her like disciples before their rabbi. Her interviews with editors of the leading newspapers and her many appearances on American television were brilliant exercises in advocacy for Israel. Her ability to mobilize American Jewry for political struggles and her profound understanding of the moods of the American people were among our greatest assets.

A further injustice to Meir is the interpretation that was given to her declaration in political debates that "There is no such thing as a Palestinian people." This allegation does not take into account the background and context prevalend at the time, and ignores the climate in the country at it was then. We should bear in mind that in that period, this phrase was widely adopted and quoted in educated public discourse, and only much later did people begin to pillory her for having used it. When she first uttered the statement, hardly anyone objected, and it should be considered tactical "ammunition" for dealing with the broadsides of foes questioning or denying the State of Israel's right to exist. I interpret Meir's remark as her signal that for our enemies to deny the existence of the Jewish state without our challenging their right to exist as a nation is inconceivable. Moreover, Meir stated her position on the Palestinian question at a meeting of the Labor Party executive on April 12, 1973 as follows: "We Israelis do not presume to determine whether there is or is not such a thing as a Palestinian entity. It is the right of the Arabs themselves to make such a determination." As for the future of the West Bank, Meir said: "The border between Jordan and Israel must be a subject for negotiation between our two countries. The Gahal and National Religious Parties want all of Judea and Samaria to be Israeli. I, however, have repeated my serious reservations about adding six hundred thousand Arabs to Israel's population, out of my desire to preserve the Jewish character of the state." She added: "Were we to reach an agreement between Israel and Hussein on every issue, including the territorial one, then taking a stand on the internal matters of the Arab state bordering Israel to the east would be none of our business. And if a state called Palestine were to be established, of course we would agree to such a state (or entity) joining Jordan in a confederation or federation."

The most outstanding individual among all who took issue with Meir's political perceptions was Aryeh "Lova" Eliav, who, as a result, felt it his duty to resign as General Secretary of Mapai. Together with others, among them Major-General Mati Peled and Meir Pa'il, he established contacts with Dr. Sirtawi, who was the head of the moderates in the Palestine Liberation Organization (PLO) and was murdered by extremists. Eliav's book, *The Deer Land*, challenged government policy of that period. Upon his resignation from Mapai, together with some other people, he founded a new party named Sheli, the heads of which won Knesset seats, and he worked to popularize their viewpoint, which called for improving ties with the Palestinians and seeking a basis for the resolution of our conflict with them.

Golda Meir's meeting and conversation with Anwar Sadat, at his request, during his visit to Israel, although she was then no longer prime minister, testifies to the change that had come about in her political position. When Sadat asked her why she had not agreed to begin negotiations when he had announced his willingness, she answered that she didn't believe in the sincerity of his announcement. There is no doubt that she too would have stridden down the path of peace, had she remained prime minister. She gave her full support to the policy of Yitzhak Rabin in his first term as prime minister, on the separation of Israeli and Egyptian forces after the Yom Kippur War, and was in complete agreement with him that such a move was likely to break the impasse and provide a basis for negotiations for a peace agreement with Egypt. Indeed, the peace agreement with Egypt that was ultimately attained by the Begin government would never have been possible without the reversal that came about during the war: the crossing of the Suez Canal, the encircling of the Egyptian Third army, and the IDF's seizure of the Canal's west bank to a distance of one hundred kilometers from Cairo. Golda Meir's share in these great military achievements was also considerable—the political and public support she gave to the army, the enlistment of American military aid in the form of weapons and planes, and the fending off of the Soviet Union's pressures and threats of massive intervention in the war if the IDF didn't withdraw from Egyptian territory.

Instead of being a source of pride for Israel, this great leader, to whom few women throughout history can be compared, became a punching bag, one more manifestation of our wretched custom to delight in shattering myths—and the exemplary character of our leaders and heroes.

History will judge her and will accord her her rightful place in the pantheon of the paragons of our nation.

Voluntary Activity in the Defense Ministry and the Purchase of Over Two Hundred 155-Caliber Howitzer Cannons at the Height of The War of Attrition

On one of my flights from Europe to Israel I met Amos Manor, who was then head of the Shabak (Hebrew acronym for General Security Services), and I told him about the business and social relations I had developed in Europe with German industrialists and several scientists in the course of my activities in Germany. One of these scientists—his code name was Ayalon—worked in his chemical plant on the development of very special materials. In one of our meetings, Ayalon told me about a test conducted by the American air force in Germany. One of the materials his plant produced was among those tested. I told Amos Manor that I thought the IDF, especially its air force, might also be interested in these tests.

Manor was impressed by what he heard, and he offered to introduce me to the head of a newly established unit in the Ministry of Defense with which I was not familiar. My collaboration with the Defense Ministry dates from this meeting, and my business interests, which involved frequent trips to Germany and other European countries, provided an ideal cover for the activity that that collaboration produced. In this way I got to know intimately many of the dedicated people connected with the Defense Ministry who had a hand in what was achieved in many classified areas and in the development of the IDF's means of combat.

In Egypt's War of Attrition against Israel along the Suez Canal, the Egyptians enjoyed the advantage of their superior artillery forces. Actually, Egypt's strategy was focused on shooting a large number of cannons along the length of the canal. The advantage resulted from the fact that the Egyptian army's organization and ordnance were based on the Soviet doctrine, one of the main elements of which was the building of a large artillery force. During World War II, the Soviet army was characterized by large artillery forces, which sometimes had the edge over the enemy's and constituted the critical mass in the operational outcome of a number of the battles.

In a meeting, at the height of the War of Attrition, in the office of the assistant to the minister of defense, Chief of General Staff (retired) Zvi Tsur, attended also by the Director-General, Moshe Kashti, we were instructed that in our contacts with the American Surplus Authority we should give purchasing preference to 155-caliber Howitzer cannons and shells and to Model 113 armored personnel carriers.

Through the contacts that our operatives formed in Germany with the Surplus Authority, we learned of a quantity of French cannons of that caliber being offered for sale by the Authority. In agreements between the Authority and NATO states, NATO members had the right of first refusal for purchase of equipment before it was offered to non-NATO states. Our people managed to convince them to sell the cannons to Israel. (In order to purchase surplus items from the Authority, a company by the name of Hydroma was set up in Germany to represent the Ministry of Defense in its contacts and negotiations with the Surplus Authority.) To get the Authority to make the sale, we had to convince the officials that the cannons were surplus.

In a consultation in the office of the assistant to the minister of defense, doubts arose as to whether this deal could come off at the same time that we were trying to put a stop to the investigation of several of our operations, which were then going on in Germany. Our position was that there was no connection between the two activities, and we also claimed that there was almost no financial risk in the purchase of the cannons since we knew that the formal transaction we would make with the Surplus Authority would be ensured, and our money would be returned to us if for any reason the deal didn't go through.

Our position was supported by Director-General Moshe Kashti, together with Chief of General Staff Bar Lev, who considered this artillery reinforcement at the Canal to be of prime importance. Since we did not reach a final decision during our discussion at the Defense Ministry, I was even ready to take the responsibility upon myself for the security of the money—the sum of $650,000—having absolute confidence that the Authority would return it, in the event the deal did not go through.

This was on a Thursday, and the option we were given by the Surplus Authority was available to us only until Monday. Kashti worked in coordination with us and transferred the required sum by means of special arrangements made with Mr. Bar Yitzhak at Bank Discount, who agreed to conduct the transaction even though the bank was closed because it was on a Friday afternoon. The money arrived in time for us to deposit it with the Authority on Monday morning before the option ran out. The cannons were loaded onto a train and transferred to the port at Zabrichen in Belgium where a Zim ship was anchored so that the cargo could be loaded.

We were certain the cannons would be loaded onto the ship without any complications since the American Surplus Authority enjoyed a special position based on its agreements with the NATO states, which allowed it to dispense with the requirement to get a license or export permits from the country in which its shipments were loaded. In earlier shipments of ours from various European ports, loading had been done directly, without any delays.

We were especially interested in speeding up the loading, since the train we hired was exceptionally long and aroused a great deal of curiosity at the port and with the inhabitants along the railway tracks. However, our attempts at expediting the loading were not met with success since the loading was delayed by the Belgian authorities, who claimed that this particular shipment had to have an export license.

The representatives of the Surplus Authority were called to the port, where they argued with the port authorities over the issue of following the local rules and regulations. When they saw the Belgian authorities were intractable, the representatives of the Authority turned to the American embassy and asked it to intervene. The embassy people joined the effort and exerted pressure on the Belgian Foreign Ministry to release the shipment and allow it to be loaded. The dispute went on for two or three days, while the loaded train, in its full length, stayed put. All this time, we were in phone contact with Kashti, who urged us to make every effort to speed up the shipment so badly needed to strengthen the IDF forces at the Suez front.

Another claim raised in the aforementioned argument was that the cannons were not offered to the other NATO states and that at least one of these had expressed an interest in purchasing them. The amount of pressure applied on the management of the Surplus Authority was great, but ultimately the Authority succeeded in persuading the pertinent parties that the cannons were not up to NATO standards, which was why they were sold to Israel.

The joint efforts of the American embassy and the representatives of the Surplus Authority finally paid off when they succeeded in casting away all obstacles, and the cannons were at last loaded without further complications. The shipment reached Haifa port, where they were unloaded with maximum speed and delivered at the pier into the eager hands of teams from the Artillery Corps and the Ordnance Corps, under the command of Brigadier General Asher Peled.

The New and the Not-So-New Historians

My curiosity is killing me: Have those called the "new historians" ever given any thought to where they and their dear ones would be today if the IDF with their bodies and the scant weapons they possessed, hadn't stopped the Arab armies who were armed to the teeth with the best weapons available, including cannons, tanks, and planes? I can't forget the infancy of the IDF, a threadbare militia, more like a guerrilla force than a regular army. It was a motley crew, with no uniforms, wearing clothes in every color of the rainbow. Because of their meager arsenal, units were equipped with an insufficient quantity of personal weapons, and fighters had to take turns using the same gun. One illustration I can cite is of a Palmach battalion numbering eight hundred fighters, under the command of Yitzhak Pundak, sent as reinforcements to the Negev Brigade, that had to make do with four hundred rifles (see David Ben-Gurion's war diaries).

The army inventory did not include even the most basic items of personal equipment, and many soldiers in battle had to carry ammunition in their hands and pockets. I recall how David "Dolik" Horovitz, the first General Manager of the treasury of the Bank of Israel, reacted when Head of Operations Branch, Major-General

Yigal Yadin turned to him with a request for an allotment of foreign currency for the purchase of personal equipment for the soldiers. Horovitz answered, with wry humor, that since the bank had no reserves of foreign currency, the soldiers should hold their pants up with their hands. (This is a play on words. The Hebrew word *chagor* means both "personal equipment kit" and "belt.")

It is incomprehensible how historians denouncing the IDF's norms of behavior can actually believe that the army could prevail without diminishing the population in the cities and villages that it conquered, and letting those who wanted to live to go freely. After all, if they had allowed the infuriated, abysmally hate-consumed Arab population to stay in place at their rear, there is no doubt that they would have faced war both ahead of them and in their rear. The scourge of the *fedayeen*, who infiltrated from the adjacent countries and the Gaza Strip, sowing death and destruction throughout the country in its early years, is an indication of the scope and severity of the problem that could have been created if inhabitants had been allowed to remain in their cities and villages at the army's rear. The danger would have been not only of a fifth column, but also of organized combat units operating behind the fronts, in coordination with the Arab armies. The Intifada, which has been trying the country sorely in recent years, brings home the fearful risk the army would have courted by leaving the population in place, no less an existential danger to the nascent state than the regular Arab armies.

Since this edition is being written at the height of the second Intifada, it is possible to learn something about these dangers, manifested over and over again in this second Intifada as compared with the first.

If the IDF had had to operate within the limitations proscribed by the criticism of the new historians sitting in their air-conditioned offices, this would have meant fighting with one hand tied behind their backs. These historians are an unprecedented phenomenon, unlike those of any other nation. It's no wonder that the great newspapers of the United States and other countries have pounced on their writings, and have given them extensive and conspicuous coverage. After all, it isn't every day that they come across such moral stock-taking and breast-beating by an intellectual minority consumed by pangs of conscience over its people's "sins." No one could conceive of a school of historical writers in Russia or Poland whose theories would castigate and negate the morality of evacuating the Germans from Silesia, Moravia and Pomerania, uprooting people who had been resident there for many generations, and expelling them to Germany. Even the Americans and the British, considered to be moral and humane nations, acceded to the demand of the Russians at the Yalta and Potsdam Conferences to annex these regions to Poland, leaving the German nation to worry about the rehabilitation of the expelled German refugees. The German inhabitants expelled by Czechoslovakia from the Sudetenland shared the same fate.

The Arab refugees found shelter, at least, in the adjacent Arab countries. It is beyond my comprehension why the peoples of the Arab lands to which the Palestinians fled did not exhibit the most elementary solidarity with their religious and ethnic brethren, and did not consider themselves obliged to absorb them and settle them in their expansive and sparsely populated lands. Compare this to the Yishuv, which absorbed so very many of our brethren, both those persecuted in Arab countries and those that survived the extermination camps in Europe.

What would have been the fate of the Yishuv if the Arab armies had carried the day? Where could the Jewish refugees have run to save themselves? The Yishuv had one choice and one choice only: to win, or to be annihilated!

By studying a few typical, painful events, we can get an idea what fate would have awaited the Yishuv if the IDF had been defeated. When the members of Kibbutz Yad Mordehai were in retreat, after having stood heroically firm while cut off and surrounded, repelling waves of assaults by infantry and tanks with only their meager weapons while being bombarded without a pause from the land and the air, their retreat was protected by the "Beasts of the Negev" Company, under the command of Simcha Shiloni. While the latter were waging rearguard battles with the Egyptian army, three members of the settlement couldn't keep up with their comrades and lagged behind—one member who was wounded, a nurse, and another member who accompanied them—and were taken captive by the Egyptians. They were brought to Beer Sheva, where they were executed by the Egyptian army. Other examples of the Arabs' lust for murder are the shocking massacres of the convoy of the thirty-five who were killed on their way to reinforce the Etzion Bloc, and the convoy of doctors and nurses on their way to Mount Scopus.

The situation on the Arab side was quite another matter. The options open to the Arab populations were many and varied, and none of them involved any danger of annihilation. They cannot blame the Jews for their tragedy; they could have agreed to the United Nations Partition Plan as the Jewish Yishuv and the Zionist movement did. Had they agreed to the plan, they would have prevented what they call the Palestinian tragedy (the *nakhba*) and the mass exodus of refugees. In the heat of argument, people lose sight of the fact that it was the Arabs who assaulted and started the war, while it was the Yishuv that was attacked and had to fight for its life.

I'm inclined to believe that the phenomenon of the new historians will pass and disappear, like a windblown leaf, in the face of the might embodied in Zionism. It is in my eyes nothing more than an attempt at showing off and demonstrating an "independent" historical approach, a wish to pose as objective and enlightened, and a leaning towards innovation for innovation's sake. The new historians are motivated by a desire to impress themselves and those around them with the grandeur of their spirit, their bold denial of truths and conventions, their unique nonconformity, and their ability (or so they think) to cut themselves off from our narrative and observe it from the perspective of one with no emotional involvement. In so doing, they call into question and challenge Zionism's eternal values and our national rebirth. Argument and dialogue with them are fruitless. In our people's book of tears, we are doomed to live with this phenomenon. Just as there is a school of Holocaust deniers, so is there our own school that slanders and sullies Zionism and the renascence of the Jewish nation. Their very appearance is hidden, to my way of thinking, in a sort of spiritual thicket that is beyond my comprehension, and is not the product of reliable, rational, and historical thinking.

Do these historians think that the Jewish people as a whole must atone for their sins, deal with a sinister past, and purify themselves, as is required of the German people after the World War? Apparently these historians will not rest until the Yishuv falls to its knees, apologizes, and begs the forgiveness of the Palestinians.

One of the most infuriating aspects of the phenomenon results from the fact that they succeed in undermining and distorting the moral base of the War of Independence, thereby polluting one of the basic symbols and values around which a national consensus has formed and the entire nation is united. Sometimes I pity them for how dearly their spiritual aridity and barrenness has cost them: they have become incapable of being thrilled by their nation's achievements, by the Zionist revolution, and by basic feelings beating at the heart of the Israeli essence.

However, until this phenomenon disappears from the horizon of our spiritual and intellectual life, it will unfortunately manage, with ever-increasing power, to seep into certain schools of thought and educational systems, and even to get them in its grip. Its conspicuous achievement is in the fact that a number of historians and educators have become, whether they realize it or not, backers of its views.

An argument has developed lately regarding the so-called myths of Zionism and state-building, the untenable opinion that the Yishuv had combat forces and means equivalent to those of the invading armies and that the IDF enjoyed an advantage in leadership ability, and in sophisticated, deceptive battle plans. Is there any foundation for this assumption at all in the siege of the starved Jerusalem, in the ground and air attacks on isolated Negev settlements, or in the battles at Latrun in which units of "half-baked" fighters fought against the mighty Arab Legion from Jordan, entrenched in the police fortress there? What about the battle at Mishmar Ha'Emek against the army of Kaoukji, the battles which ended in the fall of the surrounded and detached Etzion Bloc, the battle fought by forces from the Yiftach Brigade to capture the Malkieh police station in the north, the battles waged in the Katamon Quarter of Jerusalem, in which a Palmach force led by David Eleazar and Benny Marshak was surrounded in the monastery at San Simon and attacked from all sides, suffered heavy losses, and retreated, with many of its soldiers wounded or killed? (The order associated with this retreat has become legend: "The soldiers will pull back, and the officers will cover the retreat.") Did the Givati and Negev Brigades have any advantage whatsoever in the battles against the Egyptian column, which was equipped with every manner of weapon and halted at the Ashdod bridge as it was attempting to break through to conquer Tel Aviv? These are but a few of the critical battles in the War of Independence, and there were many others of a similar nature.

How can historians, both contemporary and earlier ones, make claims about the IDF's so-called tactical advantage, sophisticated battle plans, or equally matched forces and types of weapons, especially in combat against the Jordanian Legion, a modern, well-trained, tightly-knit army under British officers, an army which, not content merely with the conquest of East Jerusalem, fought the length and breadth of the west bank of the Jordan River. What comparison can there be between the handful of fighters with meager and primitive weapons, including a few Molotov cocktails and one bazooka, and the Syrian army, equipped with tanks and artillery?

How many weapons could the Haganah possibly collect under the watchful eyes of the mandatory authorities and the British police? After all, the British were doing everything they possibly could to frustrate our attempts to smuggle arms into Palestine and to expose the minute quantity of weapons the Haganah and the settlements managed to hide.

What comparison can there be between the number of soldiers and stock of arms and equipment of the IDF—all on the battlefield and fighting on three fronts, without any strategic depth whatsoever and without any reserves of manpower—and the Arab armies, whose airports, reserves, and logistical equipment, services, and command centers were located in their countries, and who enjoyed an almost unlimited strategic depth? The fact that the Egyptian air force, limited as it was, bombed population centers and airports in Israel and provided air cover for their country's ground forces, is an indication of this advantage. All this took place at a time that the vital targets in Egypt were beyond the IDF's range of operation. With the exception of one bombing raid on Cairo, carried out by the three Flying Fortresses on their way to Israel from Czechoslovakia, and a number of attempts to bomb targets in Syria, the Egyptian and Syrian home fronts were not hit.

During a recent administration, the Ministry of Education adopted a modern history text containing material on the War of Independence from the point of view of the Palestinians. I'm not at all sure our high school students will really gain anything by studying the War of Independence from this angle as claimed by them. More likely than not, many young people will emerge torn, confused, ridden with a heavy sense of national guilt, their confidence and faith in the credibility of the nation's historic and current leadership diminished and severely shaken.

Sad to say, many high school graduates have but a mediocre knowledge of the history of the War of Independence and the events leading up to it. Is "enriching" their knowledge with the Palestinian perspective of that period the only thing missing from their education? Have the educators and decision-makers in the Ministry of Education tried to persuade the Palestinians and the aggressive Arab states to adopt a reciprocal approach and present the history of Zionism and the War of Independence from the point of view of the Jewish people? After all, the textbooks and pedagogy of the Palestinians and Arab countries are permeated with the venom of incitement, hatred, and the desire for vengeance, from kindergarten through higher education. What is clear is that Israeli students interested in learning more about the Palestinian perspective of the War of Independence can satisfy their curiosity simply by consulting the writings of the new historians. It is very doubtful, however, that Palestinian historians will be able to document the history of their people with the same empathy for their foes and on the academic level that characterize the writings of our revisionist historians.

In fact, the War of Independence was won not by any advantage of weapons, superior number of fighters, sophisticated and resourceful organization and planning of the battles, nor by fire and sword. Rather it was the spirit of unhesitating performance and the willingness to sacrifice all, shown by fighters who drew their strength and determination from their realization that at stake was the fate and the continued existence of all Jewish people, in the shadow of the terrible Holocaust that had decimated it in the world war. The sense that they were battling for the very existence of their people and the future of their families preceded them like the biblical pillar of fire.

All my life I've known in the inner depths of my being that our human and moral superiority and our belief in the justice of our way were our most decisive and effectual weapon without which no amount of build-up of our arsenals or technological progress could help. And indeed, the outcome of the War of Independence was proof that spiritual power outweighs material strength.

Contrary to the data upon which the "new" historians base their equation of the fighting forces, it was a war of the few against the many, "a war of David against Goliath," in which the enormous gap in motivation and human quality was compensation for the IDF's inferiority in trained personnel and means of warfare. The assertion of the IDF's so-called numerical equality in fighters and arms is a transparent attempt to downgrade the great historic victory. Even if there were any foundation for the claim that at a certain point in time the opposing forces were of comparable strength, the major advantages that the Palestinian and Arab armies had before the IDF started to gain power in the course of the fighting could have enabled them to utterly vanquish our army. What enabled the IDF to hang on and stem the flood of the Arab armies until the shipments of arms and personnel reinforcements started to arrive was its spiritual superiority and the power of its motivation and daring spirit.

Why we should have to defend our unique Zionist legends is beyond me. As I see it, these are not legends, but solid, proven truths. The stand made by a small group of fighters at the Tel-Hai settlement, cut off from the world, facing rampaging masses, is no legend but heroism of the first order. Thanks to those warriors' heroic resistance, Metulla and several other isolated settlements in the Upper Galilee remained part of Palestine under the mandate, and ultimately became part of the State of Israel.

Throughout his book, *Days of the Anemones*, which is so skillfully written (and therein lies its danger), Tom Segev cunningly and implicitly weaves a thread: his hypothesis that the British were expelled from Israel by the Arabs who made their lives intolerable and their governance insupportable. He builds this hypothesis gradually, basing it on various references and documents. However, it is a known fact that historians who slant their historical chronicles according to a specific bias in order to prove a basic theory and postulation, can always manipulate their documents, facts, and evidence to serve their ends and prove the correctness of the ideas they put forward.

Moreover, it seems to me that the British themselves admit that they were forced to abdicate their rule and leave Palestine after the Yishuv embittered their lives and made it impossible for them to govern. I clearly remember the days when the Yishuv was struggling against the decrees of the mandatory authorities and the British entrenched themselves inside their civilian and military bases surrounded by masses of barbed wire appearing for all the world like outposts on a battlefield.

Tom Segev could have saved himself the bother and many days spent in the British government archives looking for documents and testimony relating to that period. Had he but made the effort, he could have learned about the distress suffered by the British and the unbearable situation they found themselves in by reading the newspapers of the period, filled with reports, articles, impressions, descriptions, and pictures that made clear how the British army and the civil service, hedgehog-like, withdrew into their strongholds.

No objective, balanced historian would skip over these manifestations of the distress of the British government during the years of the Yishuv's struggle and ignore their far-reaching political implications. Segev doesn't even mention the epithet "Bevingrad," as the Russian Compound in Jerusalem, the nerve center of the government, was called, after it was protected by formidable fortifications and barbed wire reminiscent of Stalingrad in World War II.

To buttress my claim, I would like to cite the description of the situation in which the British authorities and army found themselves in Palestine, on page 150 of Michael Eigenteif's biography of the great and renowned historian, philosopher, and man of letters, Sir Isaiah Berlin: "In the summer of 1947, some four thousand

Jewish underground fighters encircled about eighty thousand British soldiers, forcing them to entrench themselves in several well-fortified outposts, dubbed 'Bevingrad,' after Foreign Minister Ernest Bevin."

The war of the underground movements; the masses of Jewish refugees from the Holocaust reaching the shores of the country; the violent, bloody struggles over the illegal immigrants on their ships; the determined attacks by American Jewish leaders against British government policy; the expansion of the borders of the pioneering settlement in the course of the struggle against the edicts of the White Paper—all these convinced the British government that it could no longer withstand these pressures and that its government in Palestine was becoming an ever more unbearable burden that was harming its international standing. The pressures reached their peak when the truth about the Holocaust, with all its horrors, became public knowledge and the problem of the extermination camp survivors was presented to the world, the only possible solution for which was their absorption in the Land of Israel.

In contrast, *Days of the Anemones* is scattered with "facts" that we are expected to take at face value, asserting that the scheming Zionists stole the achievements of the Arabs' war for their own independence, robbed them of their victory, and dispossessed them of their inheritance.

Segev also outlines another claim in his book—that it was no longer of vital interest to Britain to have a foothold in Palestine as one of its power bases in the Middle East. As far as I know, the politicians, the decision-makers, and the shapers of geo-strategic policy in the British government did not lose their interest in controlling Palestine after the Second World War.

A further point is that the pressures exerted by Egypt's Gamal Abdel Nasser and American and British elements in the early 1950s to seize part of the Negev as a land link to Jordan reflected a British plan to turn that territory once again into a base for British forces in the Middle East—another fact that directly contradicts Segev's version. After all, the British forces in Palestine were one of Britain's guarantees for the protection of the Suez Canal and for ensuring her strategic and economic interests in the Middle East. One gets the impression, then, that this claim of Segev's is also intended to belittle the achievements of the Yishuv's struggles after World War II against the Mandatory authorities.

There can be no doubt that had the British government's confrontation in Palestine been only with the Arab population, the British army, so powerful and so experienced from the war, could have easily overcome and completely put an end to the Arab revolt. Note that after the Palestinian revolt was put down by the British and its leaders exiled in 1939, there were no more manifestations of uprising or rebellion by the Palestinians, and Britain's only military confrontation until the establishment of the state on May 14, 1948 was with the Yishuv.

In *Days of the Anemones*, the founding fathers and the leaders of the Zionist movement and the Yishuv are presented as manipulators and conspirators. According to Segev, they managed by trickery and influential personal connections to "harness" the heads of the British government to their dream of ingathering world Jewry in their historic homeland and to obligate them, in the Balfour Declaration, to assist the Jews in building their national home. The impression created by Segev's descriptions and claims is that these cunning and guileful individuals succeeded in deceiving the "foolish" leaders who headed the British government and lured them into the trap they set for them.

But of course these depictions make no sense, since any objective analysis of the moves and policies of the leaders of Zionism and of the Yishuv will prove this was diplomacy at its best. It was characterized by a tireless, undeviating striving toward the goal of building a national home for the Jewish people as a power base upon which would be established a state in the historic homeland,

when conditions would be ripe. The irony is that by presenting the leaders of Zionism—Professor Chaim Weizmann, David
Ben-Gurion, Chaim Arlosoroff, Moshe Sharett, Abba Hillel Silver,
Rabbi Stephen Wise, Menahem Ussishkin, Pinchas Rutenberg, and
others—as a string-pulling league who imposed their will on the
British leaders and impelled them to support the Zionist programs
that were opposed to the interests of Britain herself, Segev actually
exposes these extraordinary leaders in all the power of their vision
and their tremendous personal, national, and intellectual stature.
What we have here is the Balaam story from the Bible!

Wise and realistic political strategy; patience; correct reading
of the political and historical map; distinguishing correctly the
streams from the depths in the identification of the opportune
moment afforded by history, and channeling it to the fulfillment
of the Zionist idea, always keeping sight of the goal even in times
of upheaval; pragmatism and flexibility in the various stages of the
implementation of their policy ("One goat at a time, one dunam at
a time"); and strength drawn from the great vision of the rebirth of
the nation—all these are what made it possible for them to carry
the day in Zionism's historic struggle.

I am aware that these claims of mine cannot constitute a
learned, reasoned response, which can stand up to the criteria of
the science of history written using professional tools. I have neither training nor pretensions in that direction. But I don't think
one must be a professional historian to refute today's revisionist
views. After all, all that I—and many others who survived that
period—have seen and lived through dramatically contradicts findings and conclusions based on the research of certain historians,
be they ever so authoritative.

Most important, Segev's theory is based to not a small extent
on the diary of a Palestinian intellectual by the name of Halil Sacha-
chini, from which he draws many of the references for his claims.
It is puzzling that Segev didn't see fit to refer also to the diaries and

other writings of Jewish figures, such as Ben-Gurion, Sharett, or others, at least for the sake of balance.

The image of a war of "the sons of light against the sons of darkness" is not an abstract concept or merely a play on words for stylistic effect. It is an apt and fitting metaphor for the War of Independence and one might go so far as to say it is really tailor-made for this particular war. It would be a desecration of the honor and sacrifice of the many thousands killed and crippled in the War of Independence if we accepted the views and approaches of the new historians. The campaigns and struggles that the nation endured in the face of a hostile, or at least an apathetic, world, constitute a great epic of heroism and creativity, the likes of which human history has never seen. Of course there were also shadows and failures, but these were unavoidable and do not detract from the unsullied and ethical nature of the War of Independence.

A fair and unbiased historian cannot disregard the fact that the Zionist vision and the establishment of the State of Israel were the only revolution in the history of the 20th century that succeeded, survived and proved to be long-lasting.

The IDF

We are fortunate in that the IDF and the defense establishment are a source of light for us, a kind of nature reserve, carrying within it the spirit, the motivation, and the heritage of generations of fighters—in the Haganah, the Palmach, and Lehi and Etzel. At the same time, one must remember that not even the IDF can stand by itself, protected from the misfortunes and calamities that beset society. It is our job to nurture this, our national asset, which symbolizes the unity of the nation and constitutes the sole guardian of its existence, and to treasure it as the apple of our eye. A strong army, in which our sons and daughters serve with a sense of mission, which carries on the tradition of the warriors of yore and raises it to new heights, is all that stands between us and the peril of the state's destruction, or at least a tragic rupture.

I cannot deny that from time to time bitter reflections sneak into my heart: are we doing everything possible to protect this tremendous asset from the flaws, the evils, the debasement, and the defilements which have characterized our society for the past several years?

Lately there has been much talk about the decline in motivation in the IDF and its politicization. Is it any wonder that there has been an erosion of the army's standing in the national consciousness or that its soldiers and officers are not as willing as before to cope with the challenges confronting them when today they are enveloped in the atmosphere of a hedonistic society? As if that were not bad enough, there are other ugly phenomena on the home front, such as the reluctance of the average motorist to offer a lift to hitchhiking soldiers, condemning them instead to nerve-wracking waiting, often in inclement weather.

Still more ugly and outrageous is the scandalous behavior of some employers who fire their employees for being absent on account of reserve duty, not only in peacetime, but even in time of calamity or war. The reserve soldiers are defending not only the existence of the state, but also their bosses and their families; so how can those employers be oblivious to that fact?

There is no escaping the truth that the social climate prevalent in the country is turning material and financial attainment into the be-all and end-all of life. Metastases of the cancer of materialism have most certainly penetrated the ranks of the IDF.

The heads of the defense establishment and the leadership of the nation in general have to give serious thought to the decline in recent decades in the mental powers, resources, and spiritual vigor characteristic of the Yishuv in the years prior to and immediately following the War of Independence that stood test after dreadful test. It seems that this vigor has been diminished and weakened, and the people's backbone has softened in the last twenty or thirty years. This weak spot could be seen during the Gulf War and in other trials we have had to face, and it stands in striking contrast to the public's behavior during bombing by the Egyptian air force and the Arab armies at a time when the Yishuv and the IDF did not have a sufficient number of fighter planes or anti-aircraft weapons to repel these attacks. It is true that the composition of the population is different from the one that was so sorely tried in the War of Independence. Its mentality and spirit have changed immeasurably.

But precisely herein lies the need to modify the current reality, lest the leadership be unduly influenced by the masses at historic crossroads, when fateful decisions must be made.

Back then, even settlements that were isolated and encircled, but stood in the way of the Egyptian army in its advance, continued to fight despite their desperate situation, strengthened by the knowledge that their stubborn resistance was hindering Egyptian progress. In addition, it should not be forgotten that the Yishuv's strength in the War of Independence was minimal in comparison to the power base and the resources of a state with an air force, armored corps, and ground forces, which are among the most advanced and modern of all the armies in the Middle East. Today's youth must be taught to live up to its heritage and tradition of victories in every confrontation with the armies of Arab countries.

A Reversal of Values

The real sin, as I see it, of the generations of the country's leaders is that they did not succeed in transmitting the great spirit with which they were entrusted and which inspired the fighters and the people, and did not prevent the loss of the innocence prevalent in the decades before the establishment of the state and the War of Independence. They lacked the wisdom to nip the rat race gripping the nation in the bud. That rat race brought about the reversal of our values and the dominance of the destructive chase after materialism as a status symbol and prime objective, a process that entailed the widening of the gaps between the different strata of society.

There is no greater danger to the existence of the nation than the destructive social and economic schism. The social and economic gaps between the various social groups of the population are a malignant blight threatening the existence and future of the nation even more than the security dangers. The curse of unemployment and the abject poverty of broad segments of the nation cannot but undermine the wholeness and unity of the people and sow existential despair in the hearts of the distressed.

But the blame for this plague is not exclusively the leadership's. The responsibility also rests at the doorstep of the upper echelons of the population, the large concerns, the banks' investment companies, the tycoons, real estate magnates, importers, and the up-and-coming of various stripes. Today the true Israeli elite faces a problem of supreme national importance: to fill the spiritual vacuum, the lack of values, and to voluntarily undertake steps to change the situation. The sense of national and social responsibility obligates the wealthy to direct part of their resources and capital towards the creation of jobs, as well as support for settlements and for strata of society prone to distress.

It would be fitting and proper to leave to foreign investors the purchase of the assets, government companies, and other "plums" being sold off in the privatization process, and instead to focus on the war against unemployment. To our sorrow, it can be said of the business elements that their main preoccupation is not with building the land but with buying it.

Let us focus for a moment on a concern like Clal, which was saved a number of times from crises threatening its existence, thanks to the assistance of Finance Minister Sapir, so that it could begin to prosper again. Does such a concern have to its credit the establishment of new plants or businesses in any development areas at all? Has it ever deviated from its policy of buying and gaining control only of existing, profitable businesses? I published an article in *Haaretz* in the early 1970s on this phenomenon under the headline "A Robot Without a Purpose." Clal's spokesman responded with an article that appeared in the *Jerusalem Post*. Clal's purpose is "the maximalization of profits," its sole *raison d'être*.

Has the Eisenberg empire which was lured to open its headquarters in Israel by numerous tax breaks approved by the Knesset, ever set up a single new factory? They doctored stock issues and the raising of capital from Israeli citizens on the stock exchange for the Ata textile plant, symbolizing by its khaki products the pioneering past of the country, and ultimately brought about the closure of the plant and the dismissal of its workers. The plant's stocks were then eliminated from trading on the stock exchange. The late billionaire Ted Arison, who bought up businesses that were profitable, cannot be credited with any pioneering work in economically depressed areas. Similarly, the Israel Corporation also adopted the policy of buying existing companies and commercial entities without ever establishing even a single new plant.

There are exceptions which deserve mention, such as Koor and Solel Boneh in their glory days, which established many factories throughout the country and created jobs for tens of thousands of people. I should also mention the Federman and Wertheimer families, among a worthy few.

Social conscience takes on redoubled importance in a period of declining foreign investments and the creation of sources of livelihood and employment is likewise doubly important in a period of economic depression that turns the wheels of the country's history back many years.

Let the upper classes not forget that their enormous capital, wealth, and income are the fruit not only of their efforts and personal talents. They drew a significant portion of their wealth from public money; the state invested huge sums from its citizens' tax revenues and from contributions and grants from governments, Jewish communities in the Diaspora, and philanthropists, to create an infrastructure and environment friendly to their investments, easing their path to wealth. Let the tycoons not forget either the price that the nation paid to establish the state, for the sake of its security throughout the years of its existence.

Market economics does not mean "Every man for himself." Democratic society can only thrive if it safeguards the basic rights of the citizen, and the right to live in dignity is one of those basic rights. The supreme test of a democratic society is its human and national solidarity and the lifestyle of all the segments of its people.

We have no choice but to ask ourselves: Is this the nation and the society envisioned by the best of our sons, who sacrificed, and are still sacrificing, their lives and their families' happiness every day for that nation? Is this what the tens of thousands of injured and crippled, in body and in spirit, aspired to when they gave all that was dear to them for the security of the state?

When Jews immigrate to Israel from the Diaspora, is Zionism's work over? Isn't it emblazoned on the standard of Zionism that the state absorb the immigrants and plant them in the soil of the homeland, and make them a people standing proud, vital and productive? Is society exempt from offering appropriate aid and rehabilitation to army veterans after their discharge, including financing higher education for them, like any enlightened nation?

All these obligate the state, society, and all who have the ability, to shoulder together the burden of freeing society from its distress, if they want to live in a prosperous and united country, free of potentially destructive social tensions.

All that is left for us to hold on to is the hope that our youth who serve in the IDF and many of whom, alas, are called upon to sacrifice their lives in defense of the country, will cling to the spirit of brotherhood upon which the Jewish state was built. Students, soldiers, people of the working world and academia should all be inspired to volunteer and exert themselves for the public good in the pioneering spirit of those who dedicated themselves to making the Zionist dream come true. Those who are loyal to the ethical and social values bequeathed to us by our forebears should blossom into a new leadership that will lead the way and become a truly magnificent model of how they conduct their lives and in the modesty and simplicity of their ways. They should be free of arrogance, cynicism, and hard-heartedness; responsive to the people, directing their efforts toward creating a society free from the oppression of a bureaucracy that embitters our lives. This leadership should be molded from the various ethnic groups and immigrants whose experiences create a deeply rooted feeling of equality, mutual responsibility, and solidarity.

Some might say this is a utopian vision, while others will call it an illusion. Still, it seems to me that it is no delusion, nor a shot in the dark. We can already see the first buds of such a movement today in the growth of movements infused with this spirit. I need not list the many volunteer organizations and initiatives in the areas of education and aid to the needy, terminally ill, including many to help those on the verge of starvation and despair.

This magnificent and encouraging phenomenon indicates that a spirit of volunteerism and profound social commitment has inspired the nation, a spirit that is rooted in the period of Zionism's idealism and in the heritage of the Jewish people. It is my hope that it helps to develop a leadership that will unite the groups working in isolation and transform them into a force that will shape a social agenda to galvanize the nation. In short—a movemet of revival among the people.

Appendix A

Eliyahu Sacharov
120 Eshel Street
Herzliya Pituah

To
General Eytan Ben-Eliyahu
Commander of the Air Force   4.8.98

To begin with, I would like to confess that the urge to write to you after such a long delay stems from a feeling of "indebtedness" that has accompanied me since the conference held to mark the publication of the book *Aerial Railway to Independence*, in which I had the privilege to participate. Permit me to mention, to my credit, that after the conference I tried several times to call you on the phone but did not find you at home.

In fact, however, I don't have any reason to regret this delay, because in the meantime I managed to read the book with great interest. The reading added new dimensions and a wider perspective, enabling better appreciation of the importance of the event.

Right from the start, I was drawn deeply into the depiction of the events, the documentation, papers, protocols, records, broadcasts and diagrams that breathed life into the initial period of air transport. There is no doubt that the enormous effort invested in the editing and writing of the fascinating chapters by those who took part in this glorious historic undertaking are highly praiseworthy.

The book makes very clear the part played by Major Avi Cohen as the leader, and the one who placed his personal stamp on this wondrous chapter—undoubtedly the most remarkable in the War of Independence—both as the architect and the builder laying the brickwork for the erection of this magnificent edifice. Indeed, it can be said about the whole project that it is historical writing at its best.

In addition, I must say that I was highly impressed by the lectures delivered at the conference, and in particular by the interesting and enlightening lectures given by Avi, Dani Shimshoni, as well as the head of the branch, and your remarkable speech at the end of the event.

Above all, I see in this book a kind of monument to the Mahal volunteers in the Air Force—both Jewish and non-Jewish—who stretched out their hands to help our nation when it was under siege and fighting for its life.

As one who was sent by the Minister of Defense, David Ben-Gurion, the chief of the haganah (Galili) and the Chief of Staff of the Armed Forces (Dori) to pave the way for the first military aircraft, the Messerschmitts, and who stood at the head of the group that organized the aerial railroad from the airfield Zatech in Czechoslovakia (with the assistance of Levi Argov, who had been appointed as commander of the airfield) and Yehuda Ben-Horin (who had been placed at the helm of the "Balak" flights), I have, since the War of Independence, felt that their activities, dedication and contribution have not been properly recognized and documented. It was they who rolled back the attack by the Arab armies and the Israeli Arabs who aimed to destroy the Yishuv, and they who played an important role in achieving victory after the Israel Defence Forces (IDF) went from containment battles to assaulting and defeating the Arab armies.

The book relates the great human drama of conscripting pilots, engineers, technicians, and navigators from all the corners of the world, men of heart and men of conscience, who were ready to sacrifice their lives and to stand up to pressures and threats by governments and regimes. They were not deterred from joining the Israeli fighters, and some were even arrested when they made emergency landings at airfields on their route to Israel.

We must not permit the heroism and sacrifice of the anonymous and unknown—who delivered the instruments of battle to the fighters, mostly military aircraft (Messerschmitts and Spitfires), transport planes (C-46 and other models), and the Flying Fortresses (B-17) (which were smuggled by them from the United States) at a time when nascent Israel was fighting with its back to the ocean—to be plunged into the abyss of the forgotten.

It must be remembered that these few provided the nation with war material that was of vital and critical importance, and that enabled it to emerge victorious.

Their heroic actions will be inscribed for many generations in the pages of the history of the State and the Jewish people; the remembrance of those who sacrificed their lives, the fallen who gave up their souls in the War of Independence, will remain with us forever.

I may be forgiven in noting that I was among the first Israelis privileged to welcome these wonderful people at the Zatech airfield and to be their commander during those days full of dread and glory at the beginning of the War of Independence. Together we planned the establishment of the aerial railroad which became a logistical system that in the shortest possible time provided for the needs of the Air Force and of the fighting units on the various fronts. I also had the opportunity to get to know them when I secretly brought Flying Fortresses from the United States at a later stage.

It is impossible not to recall the heroic operations in the bombing of airfields, fortifications and military camps and the attacks on the enemy's forces from civilian transport planes not intended for military operations, at a time when the Israeli Air Force did not yet have fighters and bombers with the power and in the quantity required to carry out such missions.

To understand the daring and willingness to sacrifice that was intrinsic to these endeavors, we must consider the "underground" conditions in which the aerial railroad functioned: the hostile relationship of the British government, the violation of United Nations orders to its member nations, and the "detective eyes" that were checking on their activities. In particular, the American Federal police and the Foreign Ministry tried to put obstacles in their way at a time of emergency landings by planes en route from Zatech to Israel, and even to arrest pilots, put them on trial and condemn some of them to prison terms on their return to the United States at the end of the War of Independence.

I cannot conclude this letter without mentioning the central role played by the American pilot Sam Pomerantz, of blessed memory, who fell in a Spitfire aircraft on his way to Israel. He was a treasure trove of engineering knowledge and professional experience in anything connected with the operation and maintenance of airplanes, earning the nickname "Walking Encyclopedia." There was hardly an activity or operation in those early days that did not bear the fingerprints of this amazing man, and it would not be an exaggeration to describe him as a leader and a symbol—second only to Al Schwimmer—to all the *Mahal* people and to those who took part in the establishment of the transport section of the Air Force and other branches, mainly air battle squadrons.

Thus I am happy that this glorious chapter has found appropriate and well-deserved expression in the book and that the names of all the Mahal volunteers who participated in this exceptional chapter of history have been mentioned.

I would be grateful to you if you would extend my congratulations to all those involved in the editing of the book, and above all to Major Avi Cohen.

Yours, in friendship,
Eliyahu Sacharov

Appendix B

February, 18 1969

Dear Eliyahu,

I was happy to receive the photocopies of your letter, which took me back to the period when your great deeds created the fighting air arm of the future State of Israel, at a time when even the smallest decisions were fateful.

I consumed the letters (during a recent bout of reading) and I once again experienced the emotions of those days, those earthbound battlefields, where fear of the enemy's control of the air space accompanied us every step of the way.

It was my lot to endure the emotional experiences of those days when we waited with bated breath for assistance from the air in the battle for Ashdod.

At that twilight hour, we were prepared for a night attack on positions in the Ashdod area, and we were notified that the attack would be preceded by an air strike from the Messerschmitts in their first appearance. And behold, they appeared like storm clouds, and we cheered them on with an excitement that I will not forget for the rest of my life.

With enormous pain we watched one of them plummet after it was hit by enemy fire, but a turnabout had occurred in the rows of the enemy, who became aware that the days were over when they did not have to worry about the danger of competition and attack from the air. In our hearts, we knew that the time had arrived when, in addition to our own efforts, even the skies would fight for us.

Reading your letter brings back the experiences of that great era and lends them additional depth; for this, please accept my thanks.

With best wishes,

NAHUM SARIG
Commander of the Negev Brigade of the Palmach
In the War of Independence